"Outside the Revolution; Everything":

A Redefinition of Left-Wing Identity
in Contemporary Cuban Music Making

"Outside the Revolution; Everything":

A Redefinition of Left-Wing Identity in Contemporary Cuban Music Making

Tom Astley

Winchester, UK
Washington, USA

First published by Zero Books, 2012
Zero Books is an imprint of John Hunt Publishing Ltd., Laurel House, Station Approach,
Alresford, Hants, SO24 9JH, UK
office1@jhpbooks.net
www.johnhuntpublishing.com
www.zero-books.net

For distributor details and how to order please visit the 'Ordering' section on our website.

Text copyright: Tom Astley 2011

ISBN: 978 1 78099 409 3

A CIP catalogue record for this book is available from the British Library.

Design: Stuart Davies

Editor: Mariley Reinoso Olivera

Printed in the USA by Edwards Brothers Malloy

We operate a distinctive and ethical publishing philosophy in all
areas of our business, from our global network of authors to
production and worldwide distribution.

CONTENTS

To Mariley
"If only the Atlantic was a stream
with daisies on its bank"

Within the Revolution, everything goes; against the Revolution, nothing. Nothing against the Revolution, because the Revolution has its rights also, and the first right of the Revolution is the right to exist, and no one can stand against the right of the Revolution to be and to exist, No one can rightfully claim a right against the Revolution. Since it takes in the interests of the people and signifies the interests of the entire nation.

I believe that this is quite clear. What are the rights of revolutionary or non-revolutionary writers and artists? Within the Revolution, everything; against the Revolution, no rights at all. (Fidel Castro, 'Words to the Intellectuals' 1961)

Introduction

In the often fraught political landscape of Cuba – where change and continuity are often hard to tell apart – predicting the future of that landscape is near impossible at best and futile at worst (Lisandro Pérez, 2008). Despite this, a constant need to define and redefine the parameters of the space of Cuban identity, both within and outside the island, has long pervaded all manner of discourses surrounding Cuba. The numerous momentous events in Cuba's recent history; moments of fundamental change, of trauma or crisis, have served as a catalyst to this necessity to reinvent, or to rescind upon, the very cornerstones of personal and national identities. Change is as perennial a visitor to Cuba as it is to any other part of the world. Yet (exploding cigars and conches notwithstanding) the Revolution has continued unabated for over fifty years now, establishing itself as an emblem of innate Cubanness. Despite its apparent political and economic isolation, revolutionary Cuba (the Revolution is not only the victory of 1959, but is seen as an on-going project; the Revolution is still happening) has pervaded the global political sphere since its inception; despised and anathematised by successive US presidencies, it is often seen as the last bastion of resistance (significantly on the doorstep of the 'Colossus') against the hegemonic forces of 'globalisation' (often rendered a synonym for 'Americanisation'). Many of the more dramatic moments and personnel – most notably Che Guevara - have become global symbols of resistance; emblems of the 'new left'.

However, within Cuba itself political recalcitrance, economic stagnation and the ever-present, and often traumatic, lure of the States has left generations of young Cubans who have lived under nothing but the Revolution (and even then were not alive to experience the utopian fervour of those early years) questioning if not the authority, then certainly the authenticity, of

I

the Revolution and its ability to speak for/of a contemporary Cuban identity. A lack of personal affiliation with the Revolution exists among many members of generations two or even three times removed from the original event. Such disjunction and alienation of 'the people' from an ostensibly socialist political movement is one of the chief concerns among Cubans today.

In this crucible where the need to define a national identity is ever-present, and in which the political left has systematically strangled out alternative voices in an attempt to consolidate its own omnipotence, a growing number of what may broadly be classified as 'alternative musicians' are seeking to re-establish and redefine a left-wing voice within Cuba; one that recontextualises notions of what constitutes 'el pueblo' ('the people') and what may be included within the identity space of 'Cubanía' ('Cubanness'). This book examines briefly the work of three such artists - punk band Porno Para Ricardo, rapper Escuadrón Patriota, and singer-songwriter Pedro Luis Ferrer - to provide examples of such reclamations of a left-wing voice within Cuba. Redefinitions of 'the people' pan-nationally, along cultural and social, rather than outdated nationalistic lines; attempts to reclaim the means of cultural production from an overbearing and censoring hegemony; narratives of Cuban history and geography that seek to augment the often rigidly defined space of 'official Cubanness' by recognising cultural *difference* (often made tacit in the unifying rhetoric of the Revolution), yet appealing to the notion of social *equality*, are all constituent parts of this 'new' new left in Cuba. Though the musicians themselves, and the burgeoning subcultures to which they may be affiliated, may baulk at the description of a 'new' new left, or even a reinterpreted socialist perspective – so tainted are these epithets within the real-world experience of Cuban society – in many cases such a process can be interpreted. Of paramount importance to all three musicians discussed herein is the augmentation, redefinition and reclamation of the concept of

2

Cuban identity.

To contextualise the contemporary work of the three case studies it is necessary to examine how the concept of Cuban identity has been defined and redefined in the wake of two of the most significant events in Cuba's modern history; the Revolution of 1959 and the Special Period of the early 90s.[1] Though the analyses of both these epochs cannot hope to provide an exhaustive analysis of Cuban identity, I wish to address several key 'fence posts' around which a national identity was formed/ redefined in each of these periods; issues of race, geographical locality, community, and relationships with 'Other' nations all feature. Of course these broad markers of a national identity will not have been shared by all Cubans at these times. Patently, not all Cubans acquiesced with the revolutionary definition of 'their' national identity after 1959; equally many Cubans did not feel so strongly that a new definition of Cuban identity was necessary following the Special Period. These parts, then, aim to offer something of an overview to lay the groundwork for the analytical work of part three.

Part 1

'How the Left Was Won': The Construction of a Singular Cuban Identity 'Within the Revolution

The desire to define Cuban identity has long occupied political, social and cultural discourse on the island and abroad. Antoni Kapcia writes that "one dominant, and overwhelming, feature of Cuban political culture [is] the obsession with identity, which dominates politics and dissidence from late in the colonial period until the present day" (2000:24). Arturo Arango similarly suggests "even for those who... continue to be bitterly opposed to the Revolution, whatever is Cuban remains a near pathological obsession" (1997:123). Rafael Hernandez and Haroldo Dilla go as far as to suggest that a "worldview characteristic of Cuban culture [has existed] from its inception...in the seventeenth century" (1992:31-32). Whilst the socio-political history of the island as a subjugated nation – last to be relinquished as a Spanish colony, then under the yoke of the US – speaks to this desire (and necessity) to redefine the 'autochthonous',[2] in the wake of the Revolution of 1959, there has been something of a determined attempt to 'pin down' and rigidify this national identity; to find definitions and examples of a singular Cuban identity and find that singular identity represented in everything that is 'authentically' Cuban. Part of the revolutionary endeavour became to delineate the space of Cubanness, and in doing so, to foster a unifying national identity which all Cubans either had to adhere to, or relinquish their claim to ownership of a national identity.

The Cuban academic and radio presenter Mario Masvidal makes clear the potency of Cuban 'traditional' musics as symbols of national identity, suggesting that:

5

for decades... Cuban traditional dance music – the stereotype
we all have in our minds – you know, salsa, mambo, rumba,
all that... has become a banner of patriotism in Cuba,
especially after 1959. (2007)

Such an assertion makes clear that there are markers of national
identity that are clearly recognised (if the reason *why* is not
always made overt) as 'banners' of national identity; 'fence posts'
which can be planted in delineating the boundary around a
defined space of identity.

I would like to suggest the notion that this revolutionary
Cuban identity – the notion of an authentic, rigidified and
holistic definition of Cubanness – exists as something of a
constructed space, the interior of which is perhaps not clearly
defined. However, the 'perimeter' of this space is demarcated by
certain overt markers; cultural symbols which can be given
meaning as points of definable 'Cubanness' and from which a
boundary defining the space within can be constructed. Perhaps
'fence post' is the wrong term to use - though I find it apposite in
describing both a fixed and visible marker, and a point which can
be connected to other such markers to construct something of a
boundary- for these identifying symbols may also act as
'gateways' into the identity space being constructed. One may
stake a claim to one (or more) of these cultural symbols - one may
find oneself identified by them – and thus 'gain access' to the
collective identity space within. Conversely, however, one may
find oneself 'denied' access to particular gateways where one
either does not recognise oneself, or one is considered unable to
claim ownership of the cultural symbol.

The aim of this revolutionary definition of Cuban identity was
to present a united Cuba – a unified 'people'; the socialist utopia
of total social equality – and to present it as much to the outside
world as to the population now living under the bold
experiment. Many of the contested and claimed identity markers

6

so keenly debated in the ever-present contestations over national identity were seized upon and made ostensibly ubiquitous by a nascent regime intent on solidarity (whether benign or malicious at this stage). In the Revolution's negotiations of autochthonous culture, race (particularly relationships with 'Africanness') and political relations with the US, one may begin to see how a singular socialist Cuban identity was formed.

'Hecho en Cuba': Autochthonous Cultural Production

One recurring theme that could account for the stereotyped notion of Cuban music "we all have in our mind" (Masvidal, 2008) is the insistence upon autochthony that abounds in discussions of these genres. These dance musics – along with *chachacha*, and *guaguancó* – are seen as not only indicative of a Cuban identity, but somehow natural to Cuba; indigenous and native to the island. Raúl A Fernandez speaks of this indigenous cultural identity when discussing the "rhythmic building block" of Cuban music, the *clavé* – often defined as the 'hertbeat' of the nation[3] - arguing that this, and other features of "Afro-Cuban" music have "proved difficult to handle for North American as well as Latin American musicians and audiences from outside the Caribbean" (1994:109). Even in their assessment of the interpolating voice of rock music throughout Cuba's post-revolutionary history, Deborah Pacini Hernandez and Reebee Garofalo talk of "Cuba's revolutionary government [doing] everything in its considerable power to disrupt the economic and social mechanisms it held responsible for the spread of rock and to stimulate alternative musical practices based on autochthonous Cuban traditions" (2004:44); a history that, whilst recognising the appearance of 'foreign' musical influences within the island (something other musicologists may be reticent to do), also makes clear the notion of autochthonous musical practices as a self-evident fact in Cuba's cultural identity.

This discourse describes something of an isolated region of

musical and cultural proclivity; a 'lost world' of strange and 'hard to understand' rhythm, unlike, and unsullied by, anything from the 'outside' world. It is a trope that Kofi Agawu recognises in discourse surrounding the construction of 'African' in music, which tends to be described "as complex, superior, but ultimately incomprehensible" (1995:380). Agawu goes on to note both that this esoteric quality "has been promulgated by *both* Western and African scholars" (ibid.:383), and also that:

> the notion that the distinctive quality of African music lies in its rhythmic structure, and consequently that the terms *African music* and *African rhythm* are often interchangeable, has been so persistently thematized in writings about African music that it has by now assumed the status of a commonplace, a topos. (ibid.:380)

The converting of rhythm into a synecdoche for music – indeed for culture, or even perhaps for identity itself – is a topos common in Cuban discourse also. It is no consequence, as will be discussed below, that many of these mythologised ideals of Africa are replayed as one of the central tenets of this construction of authentic Cuban identity.

Even for a country so politically and economically annexed (at least from the US) as Cuba, the notion advanced by the likes of Raúl Fernandez (1994) and Hernandez and Dilla (1992), of entirely indigenous musical production, confusing and incomprehensible in its exoticism to the 'outside world' is a spurious claim, one that reveals a telling ideological construction of a Cuban identity post-Revolution, one that sought to reject the overbearing influence precisely of the United States. The spectre of subjugation led to the desire to construct a self-contained version of a self-made identity. In her theoretical analysis of such a process, Doreen Massey's description succinctly sums up Cuban culture post-Revolution:

Cultures which felt themselves to be under threat would conduct a kind of archaeology in search of origins, a search for what was 'authentic' and essential to that cultural formation. Imagined geographically, such a culture was understood as preserving its authenticity though closure. It was not invaded by cultural intrusions (foreign elements) from outside. In such a geographical imagination of a culture there would be a clear distinction between what was 'local' and what came from outside. (1998:123)

Obviously the post-Revolution foreign 'Other' wishing to invade and sully essential Cuban culture was the US. As Raúl Fernandez notes it is a trait common to many nations in the Americas. "Latin Americans define themselves with reference to the presence and vicinity of the Colossus of the North" (1994:111). The scant ninety miles of the Straits of Florida, in conjunction with the overly 'familiar' nature of Platt Amendment US-Cuban relations – "familiar to every Cuban schoolchild for more than a century... evok[ing] the humiliation of the settlement imposed on Cuba at the close of the US occupation" (Richard Gott, 2004:110) - the 'Colossus' has weighed heavy in the self-definition of Cuban identity.

Indeed, as Louis Perez notes, the space of Cuban identity was often defined by this colossal neighbour in the period between independence and Revolution:

[The] images Cubans sought to negate[4] were precisely the ones that succeeded in representing Cuba as a commodity. The contest for control of representation and self-identity was rarely easy and almost never won... if the United States served as the place of personal fulfilment and professional accomplishment, it was necessary to conform to what popular tastes and market forces proclaimed 'Cuban to be'. (1999:215)

So in the vehement assertion of autochthony that pervades Cuban musical discourse, there is an attempt to distance the island from its American-inflected history; to mark the Revolution as a schism that simultaneously broke from, and reclaimed, the past. Perez again makes this clear when asserting of the root-and-branch socio-political reorganisation that the Revolution undertook that:

Almost all government... at all levels, was stigmatized by association with the discredited [Batista] regime... That the United States played so prominent a part in this discredited past all but guaranteed a day of reckoning. And, indeed, many of the early reform measures were designed as much to reduce the capacity of the United States to continue to function as a power contender as they were to improve Cuban living conditions. (2003:239)

The Revolution presented a Cuba that had not only excised the 'Yankees' from its contemporary political and cultural landscape, but had wiped all memory of U.S. influence from its identity too. Robin Moore notes that musical expression was one key area in which this cultural cull was most eagerly played out:

The leadership of the late 1960s... focussed on culture and the media as the most central site of future conflicts with the capitalist world. As part of a new ideological offensive they began to condemn everything associated with the United States and Western Europe as corrupt and contaminated (Aria, 1982:28); this is the period that witnessed the censorship of most rock, jazz and other North American music from radio and television. (Moore, 2003:16-17)

A poignant allusion to this excision of "discredited past" in favour of promoting a 'pure history' is given in the Cuban film

"Chico y Rita" (Trueba, Errando and Mariscal, 2010). On returning to Havana, and the nascent Revolution, the titular protagonist - piano player and composer Chico - is told his jazz band concert at the Riviera Hotel is cancelled: "they don't like this kind of music anymore. Jazz is considered imperialist. It's the enemy's music!" laments a hotel worker. And in that sense, it was necessary to 'reclaim' another strand of Cuba's history, and present it as integral to a newly self-defined (and all-encompassing) Cuban identity; one that would further distance the island from the Colossus to the North.

"The Blood of Africa": An 'Other' Root

To define this distance from the United States, constructions of Cuban identity turned to a remembrance of, as Kofi Agawu defines it, "one of [the] most cherished sources of fantasy and imaginative play" (1995:384): Africa. Cuba, a nation which, as with all nations in the Americas, has had (and continues to have) severe problems with racism (Sujatha Fernandes, 2003, de la Fuente, 2001, Chacón Núñez, 2009) began to embrace 'Africanness', emboldening this facet of national history as a candidate for Cuba's 'authentic heritage' as opposed to its sullied Platt Amendment recent history and it anathematic epoch as a Spanish colony. This reclamation of and realignment with 'Africa' was partly designed to help solidify the Revolution's position in opposition to the two erstwhile colonialist forces in the island's history.

In this manner, Hernandez and Dilla assert that one of the central tenets of the "worldview characteristic of Cuban culture" has been the "early and active African component of national identity" (1992:31-32). Certainly musically, the prefix 'Afro' seems almost inextricably attached to the word 'Cuban', and as Fidel Castro himself made clear, in typically bombastic terms, at a public speech in 1975, 'Africa' holds a central place in the identity not only of the nation, but, apparently, of *all* its inhabitants:

> We should tell the Yankee's that they should not forget... we
> are an Afro-Latin country... The blood of Africa runs
> abundantly through our veins. (in Pacini Hernandez 1998:114)

The assertive rallying cry of a nationwide African root to identity can be found in such Cuban proverbs as *"el que no tiene de Congo, tiene de Carabalí"* ("he who does not have[5] from the Congo, has from the Carabali"). However, whilst extolling the 'Africanness' inherent in *all* Cuban identity, the Revolution simultaneously supposedly heralded the notion of the 'colourless society'. The issue of *race* and its role within the space of 'authentic' Cuban identity has a much more chequered past. The Cuban journalist Lourdes Chacón Núñez points out that whilst "there is no institutionalized racism in Cuba, according to article 42 of the constitution... racism is part of the Cuban mindset and defines Cubans' social and cultural self-perceptions" (2009:37). This assertion seems to sit fairly uncomfortably with the 'official' account of views of a nation who take such pride in their 'African blood'. As Sujatha Fernandes points out, in the utopian fervour of the revolution, "it was considered unpatriotic to speak of race, or to identify oneself in racial terms, rather than as just Cuban" (2003:584).

There can be little doubt that the 'African' Castro extolled in his hyperbolic discourse was at least in part politically motivated, aimed as much at delineating what Cuba is *not* as confirming what it is. The group to whom the assertion is made is crucial. Castro, in front of "more than 1.2 million Cubans" (Pacini-Hernandesz, 1998:114) in attendance at this speech, is talking (albeit in a pejorative manner) to the United States; it is, one could argue, the US that he is trying to convince as much as the Cuban population. Alejandro de la Fuente picks up on the concept of politicisation of race within Cuba, suggesting that the idea of 'Africanness' being a central part of Cuba's national identity has been a "formidable ideological weapon against the United States" (2001:18). Of course, in the nascent days of Cuba's Revolution in the early sixties, the United States was embroiled in a bitter fight to accept an African presence within its own officially constructed national identity; the civil rights movements. The chance to demonstrate to this eternal enemy that this contentious facet was always already integral to the Cuban identity was perhaps too good to miss.

It is in this manner that the 'Africanness' of Cuba's official identity was rendered as little more than a semi-mythologised 'root'; a pan-national base upon which the island has discovered its own voice (the coterminous invocations of slavery, of endured oppression and eventual triumph over cruel masters perhaps symbolic for the Revolution's own 'struggle' against the US). Pacini-Hernandez and Garofalo suggest as much in claiming that "the state's support for black Cuban culture [in the 1960s] was uneven at times. It tended to be more enthusiastic about those forms, such as rumba, that could be presented as "folkloric" and displayed in theatres and museums" (2004:53). The connection to Africa, although discussed in such all-encompassing terms as an integral part to *all* Cuban identity, was thus concomitantly presented as a 'finished' cultural dialogue; Africa was in the blood - in the roots – of all Cuban identity, but not, it would seem, in the present day. As such, discourse around Cuba's African heritage focussed upon reimaginations of Africa. As Fernandez's definition of 'Afro-Cuban' music demonstrates, the myth of an exotic 'Other' is played out with intention in the construction of Cubanness:

Afro-Cuban music... is sensual, of the senses, of physically tasting and touching. Its references to gustatory feelings are abundant... Musical tones are not tonal colorations but rather flavourful morsels, juices, spices, to be felt in ones mouth.

(Fernandez, 1994:118)

In its 'Afro' root, 'Cuba' is given its visceral, distinctly non-American, inflection.

The above is not to suggest that the concept of 'Africa' existing within Cuba – either genealogically, culturally or in identity construction - is always either politically motivated or imagined. Patently this is not the case, as Cuba, along with most of the Caribbean, saw vast numbers of Africans brought to the island under the auspices and trauma of slavery. There was also a renaissance in African derived culture in the 1920s – the so-called *afrocubanismo* moment (Robin Moore, 1997:2). However, Robin Moore suggests that this period was the true beginning of a recognition of the place of specifically Afro-Cuban art forms (ibid.:1), calling into question Hernandez and Dilla's assertion that Cuba's Africanness has been accepted and celebrated since the sixteenth century. So whilst the 'connection' to an African element of identity remained (and has remained) an integral part of Cuban society,[6] as the subchapter below focussing on race and religion in the Special Period will attest, in its politicisation of identity construction, the Revolution sought to control and delineate the space of Africa within its nation's identity, and this meant that many pertinent symbols and identifiers of a *contemporary* link to Africa, such as African-derived religious and spiritual practices such as *Santería*, were shunned (Perez, 1999). Further, the assertion that this African 'root' to identity was inherited by all Cubans perhaps robbed many black Cubans of a significant personal identity marker in the face of on-going threat of racism, exacerbated by the claim that it had been officially vanquished (Berg, 2005, Chacón Núñez, 2009).

"David and Goliath": The Defiant Nation.

If the 'return' to an African element of national identity was aimed at creating a cultural distance between Cuba and the US, then the process was perhaps indicative of another unifying pillar of Cuba's supposedly unchanging identity; the "rebellion against both internal and external repression, underlining rejection of a colonial domination and a united front against external enemies as radical features of cultural expression" (Hernandez and Dilla1992:31-2). The 'Colossus of the North' in the imagination of the Revolution is not just an antithetical Other, it is the most recent incarnation of the perennial 'external enemy' that would visit wilful damage on all aspects of Cubanness, not least its self-defined identity. Thus Cuba is cast as David against a changing-same Goliath, and as such an integral part of the nation's identity becomes a defiant unity against, combined with a mistrust (even a fear) of, external forces.

One need only look at the ubiquitous political billboards[7] peppering the highways of Cuba - now as emblematic a tourist image of the island as cigars,[8] idyllic beaches, crumbling colonial edifices and hedonistic dancing – for evidence of this purportedly indicative Cuban defiance. They propound and repeat slogans of the Revolution, reify its leaders and seek to reassure a nation that the Revolution is a living, continuing process: one that is "doing fine".[9] But alongside these more positive billboards sit constant reminders of both American aggression and Cuban defiance against the US. Posters decrying the failed invasion at *'Playa Girón'* (the Bay of Pigs), and those alluding to the imperialism of the United States abound;[10] many make reference to the "Cuban Five"; five 'heroes' of the Revolution, convicted of espionage and jailed in Miami. The constant assertion that *'Volverán'* – "they will return" – perhaps the most emblematic rallying cry and identifier of this supposed thread of Cuban defiance.

But if this construction of Cuban identity claims that this strand of defiance is unique to Cuba, Catherine Moses suggests that the invocation of a perpetual external 'Other', always on the cusp of intervention, is not:

The [Cuba] State justifies much of [its] demand for absolute
loyalty by pointing to the looming threat posed by the United
States. The Revolution considers the United States to be the
enemy. Around the world, the threat of an external enemy has
been a significant factor in helping authoritarian regimes stay
in power. (Moses, 2000:12)

The insistence upon defiance against this ever-changing, though
always present, external enemy is a trope that seeks firstly to link
the most celebrated aspects of Cuba's history. By invoking the
proximity of this 'external enemy', the revolutionary government
assumed a position of protectorate of the island, and thus staked
a claim to continuing the work of previous nationalist heroes. But
they sought too to further drive a wedge, ideological, political,
economical, but crucially in perceived national identity, between
the US and Cuba, and further, by asserting that the island was
under perpetual siege from an enemy bent on destruction, they
sought to confine the notion of Cuban identity to the island itself.
Cuba – and thus any definition of Cuban identity – necessarily
had to be found *within* Cuba. Such a definite delineation of
identity, drawn so closely around geographical boundaries, in
effect attempted to deny to the ever-increasing numbers of
Cubans migrants the right to take their national identity with
them. As Mette-Louise Berg notes:

Those Cubans who chose to leave Cuba after the Revolution
were no longer deemed to be Cuban; inclusion within the new
Cuba was defined in territorialised, revolutionary and
socialist values. The narrative was hegemonic in the public
sphere until the economic crisis of the 1990s. (Mette Louise
Berg, 2005:135)

Compounding the traumatic action of leaving the familiar (and familial) never to return, these Cuban migrants were dismissed as *'gusanos'*;[11] traitors to the Revolution, stripped of their Cuban identity by a process that assumed that defiance against an external enemy was an integral part of Cuban identity. If, as was insisted, the US was (and still is) the embodiment of that enemy, any person opting to live within the antithetical 'Other' necessarily rescinded their claim to being Cuban. Thus Cuban identity was confined to the island itself; further reducing the potential individual interpretations, further narrowing and politicising national identity, further increasing the role the Revolution played in dictating what constituted Cubanness.

In the revolutionary assertion of a monolithic Cuban identity is the desire to portray the nation as speaking with one, unified voice. What occurred in the fervour of revolutionary rhetoric was an attempt to unify the nation by pinning down the borders of a single space of Cuban identity. In doing so the Revolution forged a rigidly defined space of identity for the nation, one from which there could be little deviation, and in which dichotomies and schisms political, economic and geographical were mapped onto one another to cement the feeling of an isolated and singular Cuban identity.

A Grey Island, A Fixed Identity

By the mid 1970s, a decade which "witnessed the institutionalisation of the Revolution in Cuba" (Pedraza Bailey, 1985:20), this process of rigidification of the space of national identity had reached, culturally speaking, its nadir: the stagnation labelled the *'Quinquenio Gris'* ('The Grey Five Years'). "Beginning in 1968 and continuing through the early 1970s, Cuban artists and intellectuals experienced serious difficulties if officials believed their work or beliefs deviated in any way from official policy" (Robin Moore, 2003:15), this long half-decade was a period in which "socialist realism dominates Cuban literature" and in which "we

17

see a thoroughly politicized literary environment in which artistic freedom is encroached on not only by the state but also by peers, in which the notion of freedom is both constituted in and delimited by ingrained cultural expectation" (James Buckwalter-Arias, 2005:367-9). Robin Moore goes on to suggest that this epoch of rigidity, repression and stagnation "represents the worst of the Cuban Revolution in terms of limitations on cultural expression" (2003:16). In an epoch when the revolutionary government had consolidated its power, and its ubiquity in all aspects of Cuban life seemed assured, the tightly defined notion of what constituted an identity space of authentic Cubanness was never more forcefully tended to. Those who had left the island in the tumult of the Revolution were castigated as middle-class *'gusanso'*; written out of the nation's newly socialist identity, and forcefully denied legitimate claims to the term 'Cuban' as a consequence of their exodus (cf. Pedraza Bailey's account of this first 'vintage' of Cuban migrants, 1985). Music was similarly tightly defined. 'Foreign contamination' was excised and rebuked (Moore, 2003), and those Cuban-born musicians now living outside the country were denied both access to the Cuban populace and legitimacy within their birth-nation, as Eric Silva Brenneman's concurrence with Moore's rather bleak assessment of this period attests:

Between the 1960s and 1970s, the island performed a cultural genocide the consequences of which are still difficult to calculate today. (Michel Suárez, 2003, in Silva Brenneman, 2004:161-2)

What constituted 'authentic' Cuban music was as tightly defined as what constituted an 'authentic' Cuban identity, and was as top-down in its definition. The epoch also saw renewed and fervent ties to the Soviet Union bind Cuba inextricably to its ideological ally in many facets of life. Not only was there a greater economic reliance on sugar and oil trade, but the *cultural* presence of the Soviet Union in the form of Russian lessons in school, Soviet food, clothes, electronic goods and children's programmes etc. became central to the lives of young Cubans growing up through the 1970s and 80s. In this 'grey' Cuba, by design so far removed from its American neighbours, the Soviet Union had never been closer.

In short, Cuban identity as defined by the Revolution, became a singular state, tied inextricably to the dogma of the Revolution, entirely politicised as an "ideological weapon" (de la Fuente, 2001:18) seeking to present revolutionary Cuba as a unified nation, all sharing a common identity, and thus a common goal against that external enemy of the US. Very little room was left for personal interpretation or augmentation of this space of identity, as the binaristic thinking of the Revolution constantly defined Cuban identity as one rigid position against an 'Other'.

Part 2

The Archipelago of Us: The Event of the Special Period, and the Fragmentation of a National Identity

It was Cuba's links with the 'Colossus to the East' that was to herald the end of this epoch of fixedness. This second significant temporal dichotomising moment in Cuba's modern history - the *'Período Especial en el Tiempo de Paz'* ('The Special Period in Times of Peace') - served as something of a partial bookend to the Revolution. As the Soviet Union collapsed, so too did the only substantial trade route open to Cuba. The result was a time of near-famine, scarcity in all consumer goods, economic collapse and social upheaval that continued in earnest throughout the 1990s. The traumatic Special Period devastated Cuba, rupturing established frameworks and impacting upon every aspect of Cuban life, from the most quotidian acts to the most profound level of personal and national identity. Louis Perez sums up the significance of the Special Period when he writes that it:

> will no doubt be remembered as one of those temporal divides by which people experience the momentous transitions of a historical epoch. The *Período Especial* has served to demarcate the life of a generation, to persist hereafter as the reference point by which people often make those profoundly personal distinctions about their lives as 'before' and 'after'. (Perez, 2006:xi)

The Special Period impacted not only the Cuban populace, but also the highest echelons of the Cuban government. The vast political, social and economic upheavals forced the hand of an increasingly desperate and reactionary government. "Ideological

20

rigidity yielded to pragmatic improvisations" (Perez, 2006:303) as previous sacred cows of Cuban political ideology were torn asunder in radical contingency plans that questioned the socialist rigidity of the political landscape, and thus certain tenets of this tightly defined Cuban identity (see Perez, 2006, Betancourt, 1991), forcing Castro himself to concede:

Today we cannot speak of the pure, ideal, perfect socialism of which we dream because life forces us into concessions. (Castro, 26th July 1993, in Perez, 2006:305)

The result was the need – both for Castro's government and Cuban people - for a new narrative of Cuban identity, one which could help make sense of the traumatic changes the island was experiencing. As Berg points out:

The rapid changes in the economy and social structure made the socialist narrative appear inadequate to many Cubans. It no longer held the appeal it used to, its explanatory powers in the present diminished... As Edward Bruner argues, new narratives emerge "when there is a new reality to be explained, when the social arrangements are so different that the old narrative no longer seems adequate." (Bruner, 1986:181-2) (Berg, 2005:133)

The Special Period, for many Cubans, made the old narrative of what constituted Cuban identity insufficient. Particularly affected were those who had shown the greatest fidelity to Fidel and his image of "perfect socialism"; now sullied by political u-turns, double standards and unthinkable concessions. In this sense I would argue the Special Period can be seen as consti-tuting an 'event' in Badiouian terms, "compelling the subject[s] to invent a new way of being" (Badiou, 2001:42). By highlighting the lack of fidelity in the 'old event', and exacting "traumatogenic change" (Sztompka, 2004)[12] upon all aspects of Cuban life, the Special Period forced Cubans to adapt in ingenious, often illegal, and occasionally drastic ways to survive, but also forced many Cubans to redefine their relationship with their nation. As global socialism crumbled, so too did its inextricability with Cuban identity.

With the necessity to establish a new national narrative often comes a profound sense of debilitation and destabilisation. The Special Period certainly offered that. Kai Erikson's assertion that "'trauma' has to be understood as resulting from a *constellation of life experiences* as well as from a discrete happening, from a *persisting condition* as well as from an acute event" (1995:184, emphasis original) provides an apposite model for understanding the grinding hardship of scarcity, punctuated by individual crises in the guise of political repression or familial exodus. In a more abstract manner, the trauma of a severely shaken confidence in the established identity of a nation loomed. The Special Period, splintered the homogenous definition of 'authentic' Cubanness as both the notion of national unity, and the fervent ideological rigidity of the Revolution, began to disintegrate.

If concessions and traumatic events led to the necessity to renarrate both Cuba's history and identity, then one demonstrable avenue in which this 'new Cubanness' found expression was through a shift in both the listening and playing habits of Cuban musicians. As Vincenzo Perna attests in his work on 'timba' music[13], "the fall of the Soviet Union had unleashed in Cuba changes that have created a totally new social and musical environment" (2005:2). There was a noticeable rise in popularity (or at least a rise in prominence) of foreign musics as heard, but crucially, as *played* in Cuba (Sujatha Fernandes, 2003 and 2006) such that by the mid-90s foreign musics began to be understood and co-opted as distinct 'genres'. This move towards distinct genres understood in their entirety contrasts with previous manifestations of American music in Cuba which were, as Pacini-Hernandez and Garofalo state, "fragmentary... and highly decontextualised" (1999:19). Hip-hop and various sub-genres of 'rock' music (punk, heavy metal, and thrash metal) began to rapidly mushroom in popularity (Sujatha Fernandes, 2003, Pacini-Hernandez and Garofalo, 1999 and 2004). New genres of music which staked a claim at being authentic interpretations of contemporary Cuba also began to emerge. Perna suggests that '*timba*' began to incorporate "issues of race, class and gender that rarely surface in official discourses" into the narrative of Cuban society (2005:3), whilst musicians in other genres 'revived' "forgotten" genres from Cuba's rich heritage to provide social commentary and thinly-veiled social criticism. With perhaps the notable exception of *timba*, many of these new genres of 'Cuban music' paid little recourse to the established 'banners of patriotism', perhaps turning their back on them, feeling little personal connection to them, or leaving them in tact as emblems of the hegemonic 'single Cubanness' which was to be rebelled against.

However, alongside these radical reinterpretations of Cuban music and identity, there came a distinctly nostalgic reimagining of a golden past, indicated most overtly (and most popularly) by the 'Buena Vista Social Club' project. Cuba simultaneously reverted to the quasi-colonial image of itself; one at least partially defined from without (Perez, 1999) in an attempt to coax and reconfirm the benign, hedonistic stereotype of Cubanness to the huge influx of tourists now propping up the beleaguered Cuban economy. Finally, and with yet another wave – perhaps the most condensed – of migrants, the perennial boundary-made-geographical of Cuban identity – the Straits of Florida – was called into question. Not only Miami, but the very act of crossing that liminal oceanic space itself began to be written into the narrative of Cuban identity. The Special Period made that act of crossing part of Cuban identity; one which every Cuban had at least some personal knowledge of, and which represented economic, rather than exclusively political, motivations.

"Los Hijos de Guillermo Tell": Social Commentary and Political Critique

In light of the synonymising of the Revolution and 'authentic' Cuban identity, Castro's claim that the "pure, ideal perfect socialism" had been compromised by the often drastic concessions enforced upon it (in Perez, 2006:305) meant that perhaps Cuban society was somehow 'less than perfect'. Such an admission – however understated – was a fundamental sea change from a government who had previously been reticent to admit any failing previously, and it was a concession that many musicians in the Special Period seized upon to vent their own frustration.

Although the role of musicians as cultural and political commentators had been apparent in Cuba before the Special Period – Carlos Puebla's acerbic pro-Revolution (and anti-United States) songs a case in point - unlike previous generations engaged in political music, the subject of criticism for this new vanguard of musicians was not the 'external enemy' but much closer to home. The Cuban government itself was called into question, as was the tacit assumption, held since the 1960s, that the 'Cuban way' (significantly singular), both culturally and politically, was the 'right', or the only, way. The fact that Cuba now "found itself virtually alone and isolated, with few political friends" (Perez, ibid:292) made some question the previously unquestionable. Nowhere is this better demonstrated musically than in Carlos Varela's *'Guillermo Tell'* from the 1989 album *'Jalisco Park'*.

'Guillermo Tell' provides an example of protest against the ageing government by giving voice to the often vast generational divide; one that was so closely mapped over the chasm of real political power. Whilst the lyrics to the song may be poetic,

couched in metaphor and allegory, listening to the live version of this song[14] shatters the illusion that these lyrics are a hidden protest. The song itself uses the tale of William Tell and his desire to shoot an apple from the head of his son as allegory. However, Varela adds a potent twist to this familiar tale. At the climactic middle point of the song, Varela sings, with a buttoned-down calm that belies the significance and anger of the words:

Y se asustó cuando dijo el pequeño, Ahora le toca al padre la manzana en la cabeza
And he [William Tell] was surprised when the little one said, "Now it's time for the father to put the apple on his head"

The pertinence of this message is clear; it is time for the overbearing 'father' (read Fidel Castro) to step aside and let the younger generation assume the reins of power. Such a message, even one so couched in allegory would have been hard to imagine at the beginning of the 1980s, and it was in no small part due to the questioned omnipotence of the government that this message found its way into a Cuban dialogue.

What is so important about '*Guillermo Tell*' is that the implied message delivered to the audience is well understood; the veil of metaphor here is all but transparent. But it speaks of a confusing collocation of collectivity and individualism. First the notion of an entirely united Cuba is shattered by the overt-covert message of the lyric; a fundamental divide between the ruling generation and the young is played out. Yet in the mass recognition (and approval) of this message, there is a re-established collectivity being expressed; a generation expressing the same frustrations and desires. However, the strong and irrefutable personal voice utilised here; the synergy of speaker and message makes for an individualised identity. This is Carlos Varela's song, his message, his critique. The singer stands alone on the stage; whether the audience cheer or jeer, one imagines he will continue to sing.

Perhaps this is indicative of a paradigm shift in Cuban musical practice, one in which singers as individuals ceased the (enforced) self-censorship many theorists have noted exists in Cuba:

[band leader Giraldo Piloto suggests] that, in Cuba, singing a 'problematic' song in public, in theory, is not forbidden. What happens, rather, is that the media, by banning specific songs and marginalising certain artists on the airwaves, pressurize musicians into self-censorship. (Perna, 2005:92)

Artists found that in many instances [in the *Quinquenio Gris*] they could no longer voice their true opinions; as a result they began to censor themselves, avoiding controversial issues and choosing 'safer' subjects in order to avoid scrutiny. (Robin Moore, 2003:17-8)

Catherine Moses makes the same point of Cuban society in general, evoking the authoritarian omniscience the government purported to have, and suggesting that this trope of self-censorship is indicative of Cuban society in general, not just its music:

The Castro regime effectively uses blackmail to create fear and keep people from acting against the regime. If there is something that the state can take from an individual – a professional opportunity, a child's position in a good school, permission to leave the country, a dollar earning job – it has power over that person. It is to that power that Cubans succumb. (Moses, 2000:18-9)

However, what Carlos Varela's song shows is a negation of this self-censorship, a radical alignment of singer and song, and an unabashed, albeit poetic and thus ostensibly ambiguous, social critique of the stagnation and rigidity of Cuba's political regime.

The power of the message is certainly not lost upon the audience in this live recording. Indeed, in many respects, the potency of the message is increased by the reaction and *en masse* singing of the assembled audience. As the above quoted line is delivered by Varela, there is an eerie, almost spectral, surge of noise from the crowd. Some whistle, others sing, others shout the lyrics back to Varela, still others simply scream, as if unable to voice coherently their emotion. This collective voicing of accord and outpouring of emotion dies down as quickly as it begins. It sounds hesitant, yet uncontrollable, as if the sentiment had been on the tip of the audience's collective tongue, yet never voiced. As soon as it emerged, it is checked, self-regulated and suppressed in fear of retaliation from some unseen force.

The Special Period witnessed something of a negation of the self-censorship implicitly imposed by the omnipotence of the state, and led to more overtly critical social commentaries in song. These commentaries were often voiced by single figures, who asserted that these were personal opinions and refused to shy away from their "true opinions". It is a trait that lends further evidence to the notion of reinterpreting and renegotiating the notion of Cuban identity; one that took its cues from established tropes of Cuban identity, and renovated them to speak of Special Period Cuban society.

"Religion, 'Africanness' and 'Blackness'"

Renegotiations of race and religion in Special Period were further areas in which the image of holistic communality was shattered, smaller identity groups were established, and individual voices were made to speak out. As has been discussed above, though a notion of Africanness was extolled as being a ubiquitous marker of Cuban identity, this term was often more politically motivated that socially or culturally actioned. However, behind the facade of the 'colourless nation' united by an African past, many markers of Cuba's link to the African continent were denied, and African-derived spiritual practices were one contemporary aspect of a distinctly Afro-Cuban identity that were subjugated.

However for many Cubans, notions of Africanness, and particularly its collocation with race, maintained a significant and active part in their individual identity constructions, often precisely because of its potential in highlighting the still-present prejudice in Cuba, rendered tacit by the purported equality of the Revolution. And the Special Period saw moves to reclaim certain notions Africanness, often recontextualised as 'Blackness'.

One particular way in which a distinct identity was claimed by Black Cubans was through a rekindled celebration of African-derived religious/spiritual practice. As Louis Perez points out, the Special Period saw something of a renaissance in religion on the island, which the government could not cease:

Afro-Cuban spiritualism in the form of Santería flourished... The state could not but accommodate to the new stirring of spirituality... The government renounced atheism as an official creed. After 1991, it was possible to be both religious and revolutionary. (Perez, 2006:297)

Thus many of the deities of this 'ancestral Africa' – *Eleggua, Changó, Obatalá, Yemaya* – though never missing from Cuban discourse, were reasserted as being of *contemporary* importance, and allowed to return to prominence, facilitating a redefinition of the African aspect of Cuban identity. If the Revolution was made to stand as the symbol of Cuban identity (as Castro's infamous decree "within the Revolution; everything, against it; nothing" would tend to suggest), then the syncretism that Perez suggests took place between religion and revolution in the Special Period is a telling renegotiation of what constituted the Cuban identity. For now a recognition of difference – religious and racial – began to permeate the single voice of Cuba. Such syncretism is well known to Afro-Caribbean religion, so it is little wonder that it could have been used as a device to meld and mould representations of Africa and Cuba:

As [Lydia] Cabrera points out in her article 'Religious Syncretism in Cuba', what is practised in Cuba is a religion diversely called Lucumbí, Yoruba, or Regla de Ochoa the syncretically united Catholocism with the ancestral African traditions, thus creating a system of beliefs in its own right. (Lesley Feracho, 2000:53)

The very invocation of Afro-Cuban spiritual practices, and their flourishing in this period of extreme hardship and trauma, is indicative of this process of realignment and recontextualisation; of bringing together apparently antithetical shards (religion and socialism/ Yoruba and Catholicism/ Africa and the Caribbean) to create identity. But the syncretic mixture does not produce one single outcome, rather it facilitates myriad varied *individual interpretations*. The resurgence of spirituality in the Special Period both fragmented the whole, yet reassembled (some of) the fragments into *a series* of new identities. As Feracho notes of the Afro-Cuban poetry of Nancy Morejón:

Morejón explores space as a site of contestation and imbalance between Africa and the New World... [T]he incorporation of Africa into a New World context – the creation and maintenance of the Cuban Homespace – is a complex process characterised by the constant interplay of displacement and relocation. (2000:57)

Perhaps the re-incorporation of active elements of an African identity into the traumatised Special Period Cuban homespace is indicative of a process of relocating Cuban identity, redefining it and reclaiming and renovating important aspects of identity. But the result is an identity that demands differentiation; separateness *within* the space of national identity. The Special Period saw Cuban identity become religious *and* revolutionary.

This reaffirmation of Africanness as one part of a host of Cubannes*ses* was not exclusively confined to religious practises. However, whilst 'Africanness' was central to spiritual redefinitions of Cuban identity, many musicians were addressing the concept of 'Blackness'. The concept of Cuban musicians in the early 1990s negotiating musical routes that were 'more African' or 'more Black' seems at odds with the vision both the worldview and the view of officialdom in Cuba of Cuban culture. As discussed above, the prefix 'Afro-' seems inextricably linked to the suffix '-Cuban' in relation to musical practice. However, it is precisely this perceived ubiquity that drove many Black Cubans to search for a voice that could facilitate their own redefinition of identity. If, as Sujatha Fernandes notes, Africanness was adopted by all, then many black Cubans looked to race as a marker of the implicit differentiation that still pervaded Cuban society to identify themselves. If all Cuba was 'Afro-', they defined themselves as Black, and the most prominent Black cultural expression globally in the 1990s – one that rang true to many young, Black Cubans - came not from Cuba, nor even from Africa, but from the USA in the form of rap.

Along with rock music, rap and hip hop mushroomed in popularity during the Special Period. Through this genre, many Black Cubans found a new vehicle to represent their identity, one that sought to deviate from the historical 'root' stemming from Africa. Pacini Hernandez and Garofalo ask the following question of Special Period rap: "to what extent... does embracing rap reflect young Cubans' desire to go beyond (whilst not necessarily relinquishing) a more narrowly defined national identity and to locate themselves within a broader international cultural community?" (1999:19). It is a question Sujatha Fernandes goes some way to answering in noting that "given the lack of forums for young Afro-Cubans to voice their concerns, rap music provides an avenue for contestation and negotiation within Cuban society" (2003:584). It could be argued that many Black musicians in the Special Period were attempting to reclaim a specific racial identity by adopting and adapting the voice of rap to reassert a facet of an identity of 'difference' denied to them by the homogenising effect of revolutionary rhetoric.

Such traits are illustrated by Vincenzo Perna in relation to that other burgeoning Black music of the Special Period; *timba*. Perna suggests that "through its appropriation of foreign styles, timba challenges discourses that seek to construct a demonized image of capitalism, and evades notions of a narrowly-defined cultural nationalism." (2005:4). *Timba*, and Cuban hip hop both seek to break the notion of tradition and folklore that pervade the presence of Africa in Cuban discourse. Perna notes that:

Musicologists tend to define as *musica afrocubana* folkloric forms of African derivation such as the music of *santería, palo monte* and *abakuá*, but not styles with a clear black cultural matrix and audience such as... popular dance musics (ibid.:7).

In *timba*, perhaps one may discover another example of reclamation and reconstruction of established Cuban identity to produce a more representational and contemporary   and individually applicable - Cubanness. Perhaps too there is more evidence of a syncretism the Special Period facilitated. With narrowly defined notions of national identity severely shaken, many Cubans sought to meld cultural forms and aspects of identity – African and Cuban and Black and American – syncretised to form myriad individualisable Cubannesses constructed from the personally pertinent parts. Such syncretism made possible not only a distinction between Black and White Cubans, but also, potentially, between Afro-Cuban and Black Cuban, Black Cubans and *Mulatto* Cubans etc., as well as problematising and fragmentising each of these constructed spaces.

However, Perna warns of the danger of over using (or misusing) the term 'syncretism' when speaking of the reformation of 'Black Cuban identity' in this fractious epoch. He notes that:

In Herskovits' influential formulation, syncretism was based on a passive notion of cultural resistance, a somewhat mechanical blending of elements of two cultures into a third hybrid form, through which elements of African culture were retained in the Americas (Perna, 2000). What we actually have in a music like timba is an eclectic cultural mix, a stylistic and ideological bricolage... Rather than one of retention of African elements, the logic at work in timba seems to be that of a *practice*, a process of permanent re-appropriation and re-articulation. (2005:9)

Such an analysis makes an important distinction between notions of 'preserving' an African identity, and constructing myriad different identities proactively. 'Africannes' in the Special Period sought to break from the traditional syncretism model of fusing with a 'dominant culture' (Catholicism in the case of religion, or Spanish folk in the case of music) as a means of preservation which modulated both into a hybrid space. In this proactive moment of self-identification of *timba* and Cuban hip hop, aspects of identity were actively selected, brought together not as a means of preserving, but as part of a desired aesthetic; as representative of a wholly more disparate identity, one which, as with the musics themselves, "resist[ed] being framed in nationalist terms" (Perna, 2005:8).

So as Sujatha Fernandes argues, the adoption of rap by Cuban artists in the Special Period represents "a gesture of defiance that signals a refusal to conform to the dominant society" (2003:600). It, along with *timba*, became an actively sourced bricolage, one that revelled in global sources, but adapted them to forge and represent contemporary Cuban identities. Concomitantly, the voice of 'Africanness' was also given more specificity within this decade as well; made more specific, more personalised, more celebratory, more unique and more Cuban.

"Like Smoke Under a Door": Tourism, Balseros and Musical Dissemination"

One mechanism facilitating this bricolage of global cultural sources was the opening up of channels of musical dissemination within Cuba. Foreign musics had permeated the relocated iron curtain in Cuba's post-Revolution, pre-Special-Period epoch, albeit in fragmented forms, these rivulets of cultural information, described by Pacini Hernandez and Garofalo as akin to "smoke seeping under a closed door" (2004:44) were to expand rapidly in the Special Period; swept up on the tide of human movements that both traumatised the nation and effectively saved the economy. For the Special Period saw mass human/cultural influx as well as exodus. As Cubans left in their droves, so tourists flooded in.

The cessation of Soviet subsidised trade to and from Cuba in the Special Period left a chasm in the Cuban economy that the government needed to fill. One of the central elements Castro opted for was tourism. Opening Cuba up as a tourist resort (albeit one still denied to US citizens) and promoting joint ventures with international businesses to construct luxury hotels provided much needed revenue. "Foreign tourists were to become Cuba's principle source of foreign currency" (Gott, 2004:290) throughout the Special Period, and Louis Perez notes that thr numbers of tourists rocketed "from 350,000 in 1990 to more than 500,000 in 1992, and 620,000 in 1994 to 740,000 in 1995" (2006:309).

However, the terms under which these tourists came to the island were more problematic. With their much needed investment came a new wealth of problems for the Cuban government. As Richard Gott notes, "the economic policy makers... wanted an 'isolated enclave of foreign investment and tourism' that would provide the hard currency needed to maintain the social structure without changes" (Gott, 2004:290). It was the intention of the Cuban government to keep tourists and Cubans as separate as possible, keeping tourists within the luxury resorts and exclusive hotels, whilst keeping Cubans out. "Virtually all Cubans were denied access to most dollar tourist hotels" (Perez, 2006:309), and although recent changes to the country's law now permits Cubans to stay in many of these hotels, they still have to pay the extortionate (relative to national salaries) rates to stay at these hotels. The movements of tourists are similarly restricted by bureaucracy when visiting Cuba. Tourists need to apply, at the Cuban consulate, for a specific visa (at additional cost) to visit any Cuban house other than the *casa particulars* (privately run bed and breakfast), even if the foreign passport holder is a relative.

Yet, as Richard Gott details, this philosophy of inviting tourism but attempting to keep tourists and Cubans apart was "soon revealed to be wishful thinking" (2004:290). As many Cubans took (relatively) lucrative jobs working in tourist resorts, and with tourists desiring to visit 'the authentic Cuba', it proved impossible to prevent contact between these two groups. And the "arrival of many tens of thousands of foreign visitors during a time of economic crisis served to set in relief the sharp contrast between deteriorating national standards and affluent tourists" (Perez, 2006:309). The influx of tourists demonstrated, particularly to young Cubans who had not seen first-hand the benefits of the nascent years of revolutionary society, the sharp relief between their lives of austerity and lives of luxury enjoyed by others. Jamie Suchlichi suggests as much in noting that "foreign remittances and tourism have accentuated the differences in society between those with dollars and those without, and have increased racial tensions, since most dollars are received by Cuba's white population." (2000:58). Once again, there were growing schisms between distinct sectors of Cuban society – those with and without dollars, Black and White, Cubans and tourists etc. The vision of a singular, united Cuban identity was further diminished.

However, I would like to posit yet another critical influence that came from this influx of tourists to the island. Wishing to gain an experience of the 'true Cuba', many of the tourists who visited Cuba in the Special Period did so on specially arranged 'cultural tours', visiting many cultural institutions and universities, and conversed with students. Inevitably these meetings involved cultural *exchange*, with many tourists giving CDs, books and other cultural items as 'gifts', perhaps helping to piece together the otherwise "fragmentary" shards of foreign cultures that made their way into the island. These tourist-brought CDs were just one way in which a new raft of cultural materials were introduced to the island; the ingredients from which mix tapes and, later, burnt CDs were forged and passed around friendship groups, cementing smaller-group identities with common musical networks. Speculatively speaking (as much more research on this period of semi-covert musical dissemination is needed), whilst the knowledge of 'traditional' Cuban musical material was almost inescapably ubiquitous, searching out and 'knowing' these foreign imports became an active process; one garnering prestige and one from which one could begin to piece together a more individualised musical map.

The Special Period saw yet another vast wave of migration. The so-called *'balseros'* ('rafters') left Cuba in droves throughout the Special Period: "467 in 1990, 2,203 in 1991, 2,548 in 1992, and 3,656 in 1993" (Gott, 2004:299). The vast numbers of Cubans leaving the island – some 17,000 by the end of August 1994 (Maria Cristina García, 1996:79)- were traumatic enough, as traumatic certainly as the two other incidences of mass migration in Cuba's post-revolution history; 1965 and the 1980 Mariel boat lift. But to compound the trauma was the apparent acquiescence of the Cuban government in allowing this new "vintage" (to use Silvia Pedraza-Bailey's adoption of Egon Kunz's 1973 term) of migrants to leave. Amid seething discontent and riots in Havana, Castro effectively gave free reign to his dissenters to leave unhindered, as Richard Gott writes:

> In the wake of the August riot Castro declared that his government would now officially relax its migration controls. Anyone who wished to leave would be allowed to do so... Hundreds flocked to the island shores, to embark of boats and rafts. (Gott, 2004:299)

The result was a devastating haemorrhaging of population that compounded the effects of the earlier Mariel exodus in driving Cuba's younger generations from the island. It was a process that touched every family in Cuba in some manner. The exodus ceased "on September 9, [when] the [Cuban and United States] governments reached an agreement: the U.S. would accept a minimum of twenty thousand new immigrants each year... and in turn the Cuban government agreed to restrict illegal emigration" (García, 1996:80), but by that time, another of Cuba's young generations had been dealt a severe blow to its collective physical location and collective identity.

However, this 'vintage' of refugees arguably differed from its forbears – certainly from the more politically motivated emigration of the 1960s (Pedraza-Bailey, 1985). For the *balseros*, relocation didn't necessarily demand the relinquishing of a claim to some form of 'Cuban' identity, as previous bouts of migration had tended to. In the immediate aftermath of the Revolution, those that left the island were, according to Pedraza-Bailey, predominantly those from the "upper and upper middle class" in Cuba (ibid.:9), to whom the Revolution was politically and ideologically abhorrent. Pedraza-Bailey speaks of these first two moments of mass emigration from Cuba as "distinct refugee "vintages", alike only in their final rejection of Cuba" (ibid.:4). In these vintages of 'exiles', Cuba existed only in a pre-revolutionary nostalgic haze, becoming more nostalgic (and more hazy) as time passed. The contemporary Cuba was wiped from the collective memory, becoming only an epoch removed, which would have to be waited out until the nation, and thus its place within their identity, could be reclaimed. Such omissions from collective memory and identity are lamented by Ricardo Pau-Llosa:

Nowhere is the death of this once great nation ["precatastrophe Cuba"] more painfully evident that when talking to young Cuban Americans in Miami, the so-called *capital de exilio*. These children of exile seemed to have received little or no information about Cuba from their parents. Typically Cuban Americans have no idea who key figures in Cuban history and culture were... Cuban American ignorance of Cuba mirrors that of North Americans, for whom Cuban history began with the communist takeover in 1959... Like their North American counterparts, Cuban Americans latch onto talk about the embargo – regardless of the position they take on the issue – as an unconscious way of announcing that they know nothing (else) about Cuba. (Ricardo Pau-Llosa, in O'Reilly Herrera, 2001:221)

In these previous moments of refugee/ exile/ emigration, there is a distinct motif of severing all ties – geographical, and ideological – with Cuba, expressed by the writer Herberto Padilla as both a physical dislocation, but also by being physically dislocated, one's identity being necessarily compromised and confused:

When I arrived in New York March 17, 1980, I knew that I would be separated from Cuba forever. I no longer hoped that there would be substantial or immediate change.

In my opinion, exile is one of the biggest catastrophes of any age; however, it is worse for writers. You are disconnected for your natural environment or milieu and from your native tongue, and thus you are never the same again. (Heberto Padilla, in O'Reilly Herrera, 2001:211-3)

Yet heralded by the dramatic events of Mariel, the Special Period emigrations saw a distinctly different 'vintage' of emigrant. They were, by and large, younger, less politically 'pushed' from Cuba and more, Pedraza-Bailey argues, economically 'pulled' to the US. Talking of these later vintages, Pedraza-Bailey asserts that:

"increasingly, the emigration ceases to be a political act and becomes an economic act" (Amaro and Portes, 1972:13).

Although de jure the new immigrants were considered political immigrants, Amaro and Portes affirm that de facto they increasingly came to resemble "the classic immigrant". (Pedraza-Bailey, 1985:17)

Also salient in the 1980s immigrants is their youth. Most of the immigrants were young male adults, single or heads of families who left their wives and children behind. (ibid.:26)

These trends continued in 1994, with younger generations of Cubans seeking economic opportunities in the US. Such narratives abound in the poignant documentary '*Balseros*' (Bosch and Domènech, 2002) in which the rafters themselves, though clearly frustrated by the social inequality and hardship in Cuba, tend to be more economically than politically motivated. This, of course is something of a false dichotomy; all manner of social and economic practises in Cuba are at some level controlled and facilitated by the Revolution, thus legitimate complaints about economic hardship necessarily are vicarious critiques of revolutionary policy.

Whether politically pushed or economically pulled, the *balseros*, in much larger numbers, took their Cuban identity with them across the Straits of Florida. They felt that their innate Cuban identity would not be compromised by leaving the island; 'left behind' by the process of emigration. Thus once in the US, their vision of Cuba, and the place it perhaps played in their newly contextualised identity was significantly different from these older vintages. Pedraza-Bailey again provides apposite evidence for such an assertion, suggesting both a rift in the Cuban-American community based around generational and ideological differences in approach to Cuba:

> Among other splits, such as social class and wave of migration, the Cuban community [in Miami] is certainly cleft by age, by generation... This gap represents more than [a generational gap]; it is the difference between political generations (Pedraza-Bailey, 1985:21)

and also differences in the remembrances of Cuba:

> The early refugees' nostalgia attached them to the Cuba they knew, that was. The Mariel refugees' is for the Cuba that is. (Pedraza-Bailey, 1985:29)

These assertions would tend to suggest that there was less of an inclination to relinquish the Cuban aspects of identity upon reaching the US; that links not only of communication but also of identity stretched more easily across the Straits of Florida for this Special Period vintage. As a result, perhaps Special Period conceptions of the identity space of Cuba began to expand. Those who left were no longer written off as dissident *gusanos* and, by virtue of their emigration, 'non-Cuban'. The geographical expansion of the space of Cuban identity could be one of the composite factors in the globalising rhetoric seen in the above discussion of *timba* and hip hop. If autochthonous, isolated musical materials were seen as something of an obsolete concept, and the boundaries between local and global influences were deliberately being blurred in these new Cuban genres, then perhaps this wave of migration, though traumatic socially, provided a much-needed expansion of geographical and cultural horizons, without compromising the authenticity of the notion of Cuban music. In the complex cultural and migratory flows of the Special Period, not only was the geographical space over which Cubanness was mapped expanded, the wealth of musical and cultural resources available to the bricolage was augmented.

An 'Archipelago of Individualism'? The Splintering of the 'Cuban Voice'

The traumas and travails of the Special Period forced Cubans to redefine notions of Cuban identity on every level – from the grand, over-arching narratives of history, culture and politics, to the minutia of everyday life, to even the geographical boundaries of the nation. According to Antoni Kapcia, the notion of a unified Cuban voice; representative of the populace both spatially and temporally, with tendrils of authentic Cubanness reaching through time and unifying space, was irrevocably fractured in the Special Period. "Cuban culture [became] *'un archipiélago'* of individualism" (2005:191), claims Kapcia, in addition to which Cuban identity became a similar *archipiélago*; stemming from many of the same sources, but distinctly and individually defined and possibly even isolated from one another. Many commentators, Kapcia included (2000, 2005), have noted that participation in overt displays of national community diminished dramatically in the Special Period, and as Jaime Suchlichi notes, Cuban identity retreated back to the individual, familial scale (if ever it had existed in national(istic) terms):

Introduced by Castro in the 1960s, this concept [of the "new Cuban man"] called for a change in the values and attitudes of most Cubans. Allegiances would be transferred from the family to the party and the fatherland. The influence of the church would be eliminated. Devotion to the cause of communism would prevail. Man would consciously labour for the welfare of society, and the collective would supersede the individual one. (2000:78-9)

However, many of these supposedly obsolete markers of identity were reclaimed and reused in a time of ideological and identity crisis; religion, the family and the needs of the individual were all facets of the Special Period, outweighing for many the rhetoric of socialism, the nation and the collective. "After forty years of education and indoctrination, the "new man" is nowhere to be found" (ibid.:57). Of course this is in part due to the very apparent economic and social crises of the Special Period which made scarcity an ever-present concern, and physically separated families. But in part, it represents a move away from the rigidified, collective definitions of Cubanness to more individually constructed definitions. Truly an *archipiélago* of 'multiple Cubannesses'.

This retreat into individualism and fragmentation of the national voice, led Vázquez Montalbán to describe an environment in which "the newest Cuban art and literature ignore any sense of identification with the Revolution" (1998:359-360, in Kapcia, 2005:191). Cuban art, it seems, ceased to show fidelity to the 'event' of the Revolution, and began to couch itself in the familial, the 'everyday' (as removed from socialist idealisation), in hybridity and change, in proactive bricolage and the deeply personal. In this traumatic era of uncertainty, mass exodus and fundamental changes to previously unchangeable political policies, in place of a singular 'authentic Cubanness' came smaller, distinct 'authentic *Cubannesses*', tentative steps towards subcultures even, which took their authenticity from the Cubanness of the individuals within them rather than some spurious historical lineage or political affiliation. Jennifer Hernández, keyboard player in heavy metal band 'Escape' perhaps sums up this sentiment best in the documentary 'Cuba Rebelión' (Cuomo and de Nooij, 2008): "the media don't pay attention to us, but they have to realise, the music we make is Cuban music too".

In addressing the above quote, it is necessary to examine the 'space' that is being contested. For here we see played out a 'Secondspace' Cubanness, as theorised by Henri Lefebvre; a Cubanness that is "primarily produced through discursively devised representations of space, through the spatial working of the mind. In its purest form, Secondspace is entirely ideational, made up of projections into the empirical world from conceived or imagined geographies" (Edward Soja, 1996:78-9); a Cubanness that can sound however the individual imagined it to sound; be whatever they imagine it to be. As opposed to the Revolution's conception of 'Cubanness' as a singular entity, defining a united nation through recourse to historical 'roots' and political idealism (something of a 'Firstspace', again to use Lefebvre's definitions), the 'Secondspace' Cubanness that many musicians in the genres of rock, hip hop and *timba* of the Special Period imagined was individually defined and deliberately personal. More accurately, a series of Secondspaces were imagined, each one different, each one an island in Kapcia's archipelagic chain. Yet, paradoxically, accompanying the negotiation of multiple 'Secondspace Cubanness' in music, a return to a 'Firstspace', authentic 'traditional' Cuban music emerged. Spearheaded by the global popularity of the Buena Vista Social Club and engorged by the mass influx of tourists, who brought with them their own perceptions *of* and desires *for* Cubanness, Cuban music began to be re-imagined in concession to these tourist perceptions (Barker and Taylor, 2007). The romantic image of 1950s Cadillacs and Buicks avoiding ocean spray on the pot-holed *Malecón* was recreated for this tourist market (see the opening shots of Wim Wenders' 1999 documentary '*Buena Vista Social Club*'). With it, an 'exotic other' and a musical form to fit were re-imagined. Where many musicians were reconstructing their cultural identities to incorporate foreign musics, co-opting them to reflect a contemporary Cuba, the renewed pressure of tourist perception, and Cuba's place within the world music circuit began to reshape a retro(gressive) Cuban identity that coincided with its own ideals. This Firstspace reimagining of Cubanness may have only represented one of the many Secondspace archipelagos – one of the *potential* definitions of Cuban cultural identity now – but it was certainly the most dominant on a global scale.

As the new millennium approached, and the nightmare of the Special Period receded, Cuban identity had been reclaimed by many, reshaped by some and changed by an epoch that made top-down, holistic, authoritarian notions of what constituted a Cuban identity anachronistic and irrecoverable.

Part 3

A Reclaimed Identity: Redefining the Left, and Reassembling the Nation

Though revolutionary rhetoric of unity and solidarity (particularly as tied to issues of political and national affiliation) may be largely anachronistic to many young Cubans in post-millennium Cuba, in the endeavours of a number of musicians working in Cuba today, there is a growing attempt to re-establish something of a united – though not homogenous – Cuban voice. In a move away from the individualisation (and individualism) of the Special Period, increasingly difference and diversity are being reincorporated into a more complex whole; a more representative Cubanness. Surprisingly, these visions of Cubanness often tend to have a distinct left-wing flavour to them. Forging left-wing oppositional voices to a socialist government may seem paradoxical, but the work of the musicians cited herein demonstrate two key facets; one, that the government – in its totalitarian grip on the country – has ceased to represent both the mores of contemporary Cuban society and a truly left-wing perspective; and two, that a redefinition and reappraisal of more genuine left-wing narratives may provide a radical and regenerative negotiation of Cuba's uncertain future; one that steers a course between two undesirably rigid and obsolete political stances: neoliberal capitalism and totalitarian communism.

Punk band Porno Para Ricardo, rapper Escuadrón Patriota, and Pedro Luis Ferrer,[17] a proponent of one of Cuba's lesser known traditional musics – *changüi* – represent three examples of post-millennial reimagining of Cuban identity by attempting to expand upon the established soundworld of what constitutes 'Cuban music'. Each of these musicians (and more besides working in Cuba today) seem to be constructing a space of collective identity that, in its attempt to be truly holistic (that is to be representational of the multifarious voices staking a claim to Cubanness) is necessarily complex, potentially contradictory and eclectic. Punk, rock, hip-hop, jazz, reggae; all these 'imported' styles become legitimate visitors to the Cuban sound-world. But perhaps unlike their Special Period forbears, who felt more of need to reject traditional models of Cubanness in espousing their identity, in contemporary Cuban music making, there is a growing sense of ownership of these traditional models of Cuban music from sectors of this so-called 'alternative' musicianship – labelled under the broad rubric *friki*.[18] Not so much a Thirdspace, in the traditional Bhabhaian sense of the term (Bhabha, 1990, 1994) as an expanded definition *within* the already established space of Cuban identity. Tradition and modern genres are not synthesised into a singular defined space but left as constituent parts of a more complicated whole. It is a definition of Cubanness that retains its individuality, but attempts to re-imagine and re-establish a sense of collectivity and unity. Perhaps here there is something of Edward Soja's theorisation on 'the Aleph' of Jorge Luis Borges in the work of these musicians. Borges writes of this fictional Aleph:

What eternity is to time, the Aleph is to space. In eternity, all time – past, present and future – coexists simultaneously. In the Aleph, the sum total of the spatial universe is to be found in a tiny shining sphere barely over an inch across. (Borges, 1971:189)

Edward Soja uses this literary device to describe a more open notion of a "Thirdspace" that is capable of containing within it a multiplicity of definitions – or rather the constituent 'ingredients' - to establish for oneself a personalised vista. Thirdspace is:

the space where all places are capable of being seen from
every angle, each standing clear; but also a secret and conjec-
tured object, filled with illusions and allusions, a space that is
common to all of us yet never able to be completely seen or
understood. (Soja, 1996:56)

Within the politicised binarisms of Cuban discourse, this
'Thirdspace' still retains some radicalism, rather than consti-
tuting a compromising middle ground. Perhaps the term (though
not Soja's definition thereof) is slightly misleading within the
case of these post-millennial musicians, as the space being
claimed is precisely that of Cuban identity; not some synthesised
and syncretic hybrid space. In the work of all three of these case
studies, "whatever is Cuban" is still of paramount importance.
Here we see a Cuban identity capable of housing myriad
different vistas – myriad different identities; each different from
one another, yet all connected by being shades and reflections of
the same singular space. In Escadrón's rap, or Porno Para
Ricardo's distorted guitars, in Pedro's Arabic turns on the *trés*,[19]
fragments of the whole are uncovered; vistas from the shining
sphere of the 'Cuban Aleph' are glimpsed. But in each vista, there
is the recognition of absence, a partiality (in both senses of the
word), but crucially, there is the ability to look again into the
Cuban Aleph and find another definition.

However, it is not a postmodern bricolage that each of these
artists demonstrates in their work. Nor does it (exclusively) speak
of a broader global adoption of so-called 'globalised' musics
(punk and hip-hop have reared their heads in many disparate
countries around the world). A knowledge of, and distinct
reference to, the Cuban condition is of paramount importance to
each of them. In their reappraisal of Cuban identity, there is not
an oblique call for Cubanness to 'be whatever you choose it to
be', rather there is a pointed attempt to reclaim the narrow,
hegemonic definition of what constitutes Cubanness precisely by

reconnecting these broken slabs of Cuban history, by attempting to reconnect Cuba into a global dialogue (or demonstrate that these connections were already established), by renegotiating the spaces in which collective assembly and community recognition take place, and, through social commentary, demonstrating the anachronistic nature of Castro's Revolution, yet through that same social commentary, establish a truly left-wing narrative for the continuation of a more productive, more representative Cuban identity that can take its place on the global stage. But it must take its place on this global stage *as* Cuban. The process here is more complicated than a shift from the local to the global, from the traditional to the contemporary, from the autochthonous to the international; a further homogenisation of the world music map. There are glistening, nuanced cultural referents in each of these supposedly 'global' genres, belying the notion of musical homogeneity. Rap hip-hop and Latin American folk music are constituent elements in a local-national-global nexus, and sit alongside (though not always comfortably) rumba, salsa, mambo and chachacha.

Porno Para Ricardo - Sounding the Home: DIY and a Dual Definition of 'Home Recording'

at the time I started the group, I saw that a lot of [rock] bands would play the song on stage and then the next song, and there was no contact, and on top of that they would sing in English – allegedly – and also guttural [impersonation of heavy metal voice] and so I saw that there was no communication with that music. So I said 'if I want to listen to the music I like, I will have to create my own band' (Gorki, 2010)

Porno Para Ricardo are a punk band formed in 1999 in Havana; formed as much as an opposition to the mimetism of Cuba's heavy metal bands as to the staid conformity of the *quinquenio gris* and desperation of the Special Period. Lead singer and founder Gorki Águila Carrasco would listen (with some chagrin) to Cuban rock bands singing in English, offering "no communication" (ibid.); before that he had pored over Led Zeppelin and Sex Pistols records, as well as absorbing the ubiquitous *boleros* played on Cuban radio stations. The band Gorki endeavoured to form would be one that took sonic influence from these rock sources, yet would couch them in a distinctly (and vehemently) Cuban dialect. Delivering a message would be the *raison d'être*, and the band would not compromise in delivering this message: they would endeavour to say what others are thinking.[20]

The band's first album (*'Rock Para Las Masas... Cárnicas'*)[21] garnered some begrudging notoriety and limited exposure from the Cuban media. They performed on the alternative music show *'Cuerda Viva'* in 2002[22] and occupied a position certainly not of acceptance, but certainly not of the outright censorship that has dogged the band in recent years. They had a small but loyal fan base who would convene at the scant locations for rockers in Havana (such as the now defunct *'Patio de Maria'*) to watch Porno Para Ricardo's anarchic gigs. The band's homemade music videos for *'Los Musicos de Bremen'* (a punk cover version of a Soviet cartoon theme song) and *'El Cake'* were passed among this small collective, garnering a cult following. However, the band's history contains within it something of its own 'event'; a trauma that produced a sea change in identity for the band. In 2003 Porno Para Ricardo played at a rock festival in *Pinar del Rio*[23]. Following their performance, Gorki claims to have been approached by a woman insisting on buying drugs from him. The exact details of the encounter are spurious;[24] suffice to say the result was that Gorki was arrested for drug possession and intent to supply; a charge that he vehemently denies, (Maza, 2010). Gorki was sentenced to four years in jail. He served two under desperate conditions, and it is no surprise that such treatment imbued Gorki, and the band, with a fierce sense of injustice and a further need to vociferously voice their opinion.

On release from prison, the band were stripped of their membership to the *'Asociación Hermanos Saíz'* (AHS)[26] and as such are effectively banned from all live performance; both directly in Cuba, and indirectly outside of Cuba through visa restrictions. The band, and particularly Gorki, endure constant harassment and monitoring from the authorities, making even the most mundane bending of stringent regulations (a *de rigueur* part of the Cuban everyday) an unnecessary chore. The band's CDs – *"Rock Para Las Masas..."*, two albums simultaneously (self) released in 2006 (*'Soy Porno, Soy Popular'* and *'A Mí No Me Gusta La Políticas Pero Yo Le Gusta a Ella, Compañeros'*) and one in 2008 (*'El Diso Rojo'*)[27] - are unavailable for purchase within Cuba.[28] It goes almost without saying that their music receives absolutely no airplay on any of Cuba's media outlets. The band are essentially forced not to exist in any aspect "within the Revolution", showing Fidel Castro's emblematic maxim at its most potent and pugnacious. The band have existed for most of their career in the hinterland of Cuba's music scene and, tarnished with the black mark of being 'dissidents', they have been similarly marginalised within Cuban society. That they do still exist is telling. Despite this wilful campaign to silence the band, they have continued to make noise from the sidelines. Though they are not well *heard*, they are certainly well *known*, both within Cuba and outside.

Yet aside from the notoriously controversial anti-Castro lyrics, much of Porno Para Ricardo's work seeks to construct a soundworld that attempts to redefine a Cuban identity space by representing a *homespace*. The band utilise sounds of the home and of the everyday to foster connections between Cuban people that are more quotidian, and much more applicable. This quotidian Cubanness sits in stark contrast to the mythologisation and disjunctive hero-worship of the Revolution; a regime that still asserts that to be Cuban is to "be like Che".[29]

Sounding the Home: Creating Commonality by (Re)Presenting the Everyday

That most popular and influential of all recent inventions, the radio, is nothing but a conduit through which prefabricated din can flow into our homes. And this din goes far deeper, of course, than the ear-drum. It penetrates the mind. (Aldous Huxley, 1944:218-9)

The sound of the radio is often a short hand symbol for the sound of the familial; part of the tapestry of sound that creates the 'sound of home'. Jo Tacchi suggests that "radio sound creates a textured "soundscape" in the home, within which people move around and live their daily lives", going on to say that "radio sound is experienced as a part of the material culture of the home, and that it contributes greatly to the creation of domestic environments" (Tacchi, 1998:26). The sound of radio is given an even more prominent place in the soundscape of the home in Cuba, where, for many families, the radio is still the primary news and entertainment-giving technological device. The presence of the radio in Cuban homes fulfils Tacchi's espoused roles as "friend" and "company" (ibid.) for the listener, but also plays out a significant role as informer (politically and culturally). Vincenzo Perna illustrates the importance of the radio in Cuba, claiming that one bridge spanning the schism of the 1959 Revolution is that "radio continued to be crucial in orienting musical tastes and determining popularity and prestige of popular musicians (Acosta, 1990)" (Perna, 2005:75), further asserting that radio is still "the most popular local medium for music" (ibid.:80).

Gorki describes the ubiquity of the radio in his house, and the integral place the radio played in his upbringing, and in the formation of a Cuban soundscape and culture:

my mother always had a musical environment in the house.

She used to work with music. She used to put the radio on –
radio progresso –and she'd put these long radio shows on with
music – like a disco – so the environment surrounding me was
rural music and boleros and the like, and mum used to love
to sing whilst she was working. (Gorki, 2010)

A discourse that gives weight to Tacchi's theorisation on the
place of the radio, it would appear that for Gorki, as for many
Cubans, the radio is an immediate marker of the sound of the
home. So the band's decision to open their first album with the
sound of a radio scanning through reams of static to find a radio
announcement ('*Intro*', track one on '*Rock Para Las Masas...*')
would appear to immediately set up a familiar/ familial tone to
the album; one that is perhaps shattered (or at least questioned)
in the ensuing 'noise' of their punk rock songs, but one that, in a
sense is perhaps symbolic of the band's whole ethos. For here we
have a familiar Cuban sound; the radio, playing salsa and
relaying current affairs in serious tones (the sound of the solemn
news/speaking clock radio station '*Radio Reloj*' can be heard
emerging from the static), two cornerstones of the Cuban
national identity as purported by the government; a love for a
defiantly autochthonous musical forms and a sober engagement
with current socio-political affairs.

Yet, tellingly, these two prominent and instantly recognisable
'sounds' emanating from the radio (each plays for less than a
second on the track) are spikes of sound pushing through a
relentless barrage of 'noise'. As Abraham Moles succinctly puts
it, in most orthodox uses, "shocks, crackling, and atmospherics
are noises in a radio transmission" (Moles 1968:78). But for Porno
Para Ricardo, in this opening gambit, the static and crackles –the
noise – is an integral part of the message being relayed. Noise *is*
the signal. The band are literally putting the noise back into the
traditional signals coming from this familiar source of 'home
sound'; celebrating the gaps in between the stations by lingering

on the white noise between them. Are they presenting themselves *as* that static; as those gaps between the conventional messages? Or are they attempting to dismantle the traditional listening habits associated with the radio, before forcefully inserting themselves into the space, expanding the parameters of 'the radio', and thus of 'Cuban sound', and thus 'Cuban identity', to include themselves as a legitimate expression of these three inter-related spaces (and asserting that these spaces exist *within the band*)? Are they performing a Cuban sound where, if one searches through the noise for long enough, one may come across their sound, and once heard, it must be considered as existing alongside the familiar stations along this line of static?

I am tempted to read something of a less deviant meaning into this use of radio sound. Rather than an attempt to 'territorialise', recontextualise and subvert the meaning and usage of the radio as part of the Cuabn soundscape via interpolating noise, I see this introductory track as an attempt to record a 'natural' scene from 'the Cuban home'. Porno Para Ricardo, though delivered through their own unique lens, are celebrating an aspect of the everyday; celebrating a moment of shared mundanity – selecting a radio station - and recognising a distinctly important aspect of a shared, and potentially unifying, soundscape. They are not only identifying an instantly recognisable and identifiable tenet of 'quotidian Cubanness', but elevating it to a position of high importance; the first track on their first album. Crucially, the band are aligning themselves with this most Cuban of Cuban sounds from the very outset of their recording career. They are positioning themselves as coming from, reflecting and poten-tially existing as part of, this familiar soundscape, but they are also positioning another fencepost around the circle of individual/collective identity; a potentially inclusionary signpost marking the parameter of their identity, which, if one shares the significance of the sounds therein, one too can identify with. So the sound of flicking through the static of a radio, past salsa and speaking clocks, past crooning and revolutionary rhetoric, past histrionic radio *novellas*, to come to some end point (be it Porno Para Ricardo or not) invokes the sound of the Cuban home and soundscape and, to those who share in some part of that, evokes memories that can (re)confirm their individual identity, and allow them at least partial access to the space of identity forged by the band. In placing such an importance upon an otherwise mundane 'noise' of the home, Porno Para Ricardo are bringing into focus an emblem of shared culture and identity among Cubans that exists outside of revolutionary paradigms. Here is a *truly* Cuban identity – an everyday pastime – the sound of the *real* everyman: listening to the radio. In celebrating this quotidian Cuban identity, the band are bringing the private world and the public world – two very different spaces in Cuba – together.

Again, many theorists examining Cuba have noted the divide between the private and public spaces in Cuban social and political life. Because of the strict censorship of the state, the public sphere has ceased to be a space in which many Cubans feel they can voice their true opinion, and thus find expression for their identity. Public demonstrations of fidelity to the Revolution – many of them compulsory – have become little more than keeping up appearances (see Moses, 2000, and Kapcia, 2005), leaving only the very private enclave of the home – and that most intimate circle of close friends and family – as the only space in which a 'true identity' can be voiced.

By making this indicator of privacy and intimacy available to an audience, Porno Para Ricardo are offering 'the home' (with all the secretive and private identity markers it entails) up to a public forum, and thus fostering the potential for interconnection between private spaces of identity. Tacchi writes that "the wider world is not shut out when we listen to the radio in the home; in fact it has a very direct channel into the most private sphere." (1998:33). The manner in which "a soundscape can operate to link the social and the private" (ibid.:36) is demon-strated in the private usages of the public signal of the radio. In many instances, it serves to allay the potential isolation of the private soundscape by connecting it with a broader community, not only through the 'voice from without' (the singer, news broadcaster or radio personality) being invited into the private sphere, but through the imagined and tacit connections with a community who, by listening, even in private, to the same signal, build up a collection of shared cultural reference points, and thus are able to share certain signposts of identity, can recognise these common traits in one another, and thus, when represented in music such as this example given by Porno Para Ricardo, they serve as an easily identifiable cultural 'hit point'; a 'hook' which not only serves to incorporate 'Cubanness' into the band's sound, but simultaneously incorporate the band into the realm of Cubanness. Similarly, the band are attempting to blur the boundary between the isolated enclaves of Cuban family groups and the wider community, or attempting to re-establish the public as a space in which Cubans may express their 'true' identity by reasserting the everydayness - the individually orchestrated nature - of the public, and removing from it the dogmatic, enforced communality of political marches and reifi-cation of revolutionary heroes.

The use of familiar/familial noise such as the radio, but also noises from the street, helps reinforce the notion of Porno Para Ricardo existing 'naturally' within the Cuban soundworld. Car horns, shouted conversations and, most interestingly, laughter are all deliberately incorporated into Porno Para Ricardo's sound-world; but incorporated to foster a feeling of communality, of *gosadera*, of familial *bulla*; distinctly Cuban states ('*gosadera*' means an atmosphere of scandalous partying, '*bulla*' means noise, but can often have a more 'positive' inflection than the word '*ruido*') that attempt to represent the everyday. But by representing the melded private/public soundworld in their recordings – deliberately adding it to their sound – and thus staking a claim to it as part of their identity, they are helping to connect the individualised private listening of their music by sounding a series of communally recognisable identity markers. Just as the radio can help bridge this gap between the private and the public spheres of sound, so too Porno Para Ricardo's *use* of these same sounds can help form tacit group identities through shared recognitions and shared soundscapes. The result is a Cuban soundscape that is individually nuanced by sounds from the everyday, but is collectively understandable. From laughter, the sounds of the city, the radio, the intimate and personal mixing with the public to form a unity based on shared memories, moments and cultural markers, rather than doctrines, heroes and national holidays.

Silent Noise: The Soundproofed Studio and the Reclamation of Cultural Production

However, in this maelstrom of representational noise, what of its 'other': silence? Can silence be said to be engaged in any of this identity work, and if so, what does silence 'say' about the band?

Surprisingly, silence seems to come, or is at its most crucial for Porno Para Ricardo, at the moment of the loudest noise: when recording. When I met with Gorki in Prague (July 2011), work on the refurbishment of his home recording studio had just finished. Discussing the construction, he was keen to go into explanatory depths concerning the precise building specifications of the studio. Of most significance (and the source of greatest pride) was the sound proofing of the studio, which Gorki insisted upon being absolute. Therefore, an internal shell of chipboard has been installed, and the surrounding gap between chipboard and wall filled with sound-resistant foam. The studio-cum-rehearsal-room of Porno Para Ricardo, on the top floor of a modest-sized, three-storey block of flats in the *Playa* district of Havana, is entirely, deliberately and significantly soundproof.

The necessity and desire for apparent silence emanating from this most noisy of spaces is not merely perfunctory – a courtesy to neighbours. Nor is it an acquiescence to the government, or an attempt to exist under the radar, or not draw attention to the questionable legality of the studio. The desire to 'contain' the noise; to have it exist in a private and controlled space is of paramount importance to Gorki and the band. The demand is for a strictly controlled (controllable) 'home' within which an equally self-determined sound can be forged. As Tim Edensor notes, "the construction of home... is integral to the boundaries of space-making, specifying the enclosed realm of the 'private' in contradistinction to the 'public'" (2002:57-8). In Gorki's almost fastidiously detailed description of the specification of the sound-proofed studio, one can detect this desire to have absolute control over space-making, and a desire for that space to be entirely self-contained; physically but, crucially, sonically. There exists in the band's studio an entirely private space; a home *within* the home, privacy within private space. Yet it is a private space which is filled with noise. There is a desire to fill this isolated space with a self-defining, but only ever self-heard noise. And this desire would tend to problematise, as does Ian Biddle, the binarity that has been forged around noise/silence:

One way in which the sentimental materialism of noise has been played out is in the (often hidden) reliance on the juxta-position of two opposed sonic zones, which we might charac-terise as privacy-silence and ubiquity-noise. Either noise is understood to enable an emancipation from the stuffy drawing rooms of polite bourgeois respectability or it occasions a martyrolgical discourse in which sensitive creatures are brutalised by the cruel neighbour or the heartless mob. (2009:6)

In Porno Para Ricardo's desire to create an impenetrable barrier around the physical space of noisemaking - their studio – so that it is unheard by all those outside that space, they are in a sense, reversing that binary and creating a space of privacy-noise; delighting in the secrecy of their noise-making – silent noise. As Jacques Attali notes, "Eavesdropping, censorship, recording, and surveillance are weapons of power" (1985:7), and for Porno Para Ricardo, the very possibility to record within their own home – particularly the ability to record such 'noise' (that is sound that the government would consider a dissident message) is a source of tremendous power to the band. That the studio itself appears to be silent from the perspective of the 'outsider' only serves to increase this power. The band, by recording, show the government to be incapable of preventing them from recording; by doing so silently, they show the government's inability to police the private space with the omniscience they purport to possess. The noise that the band create in this private space is deliberate. It is *created*, not tolerated. Noise does not come from within to shatter the silence of those outside, nor does it flood in from without to oppress those inside. Rather, in this soundproof world, it reverberates and rebounds, doubling and reinforcing itself, made by and exclusively for the noise makers themselves.

This studio that we're building is a result of being very conscious of the price that we have to pay for confronting the government and the institutions in this country. To make a recording studio means a lot to us, because it gives us massive autonomy when creating our music. (Gorki, 2010)

The desire for autonomy from the hegemony of the government controlled music 'industry' is a critical reassessment of left-wing ideology through music. In a nation where the state-run record label 'EGREM' is still monolithic in its dominance, Porno Para Ricardo's reassertion of that most classic punk ethos – DIY – serves as a tool to break governmental control over what music is made and disseminated, and demands a reclamation of the means of cultural production. Porno Para Ricardo's home studio serves to demonstrate that the revolutionary government exists in Cuba now as a ruling elite who, through strict control over precisely these means of cultural production – record labels, musician's unions and associations etc. – have moulded and dictated what is produced. By forcefully producing music outside of the revolutionary paradigm, Porno Para Ricardo aim to highlight its obsolescence; that one may indeed have 'every-thing', even 'outside the Revolution':

[the recording studio] works for other artists that can come to record in this studio, to give them that opportunity and also to a great extent to demonstrate to them that if we could do it, they can also do it – which means it is possible to have a life outside of the institutions. It is possible to continue creation without the institutions, but people don't think so. Of course they would have to pay a price like us, they have to take the risk and they have to stop being afraid. They must stop being afraid. Of course, we don't expect everyone to be like us. It's impossible. I don't get in that critical mindset that I used to have before. I used to be a lot more radical in that sense before...

many people don't think beyond and get stuck with what is already made; that is the institution and the rules of how to make rock. ... Here there is a lot of 'mimetismo' [copying] a lot of copying of the fashion, of MTV or of what they see, and then, therefore because your mind doesn't see beyond that horizon, you expect institutions to give you everything, because it is a totalitarian regime. The government controls everything, and it likes to think that you have to do everything with it and that everything is politics. (Gorki, 2010)

The punk message of 'Do it Yourself' is rekindled and used to emphasise the disjuncture between the revolutionary government and 'ordinary' Cuban people. It offers a possible route other than that through adherence to the system, and in reclaiming music as existing in the private 'home', a newly unified public identity can be constructed out of precisely these cultural products.

Porno Para Ricardo's studio serves up a dual definition of 'home recording'. The music made there is at once a recording made within the private sphere of home, but, by incorporating and utilising sounds from both the private and the social sound-scapes of Havana – the radio, television jingles, car horns, police sirens, torrential rain, snippets of salsa and chachacha – the band are also creating a recording *of the home*; representing the commonality of private, potentially isolated, sound-spaces in which individual identities are constructed. They are replaying 'home' and 'the street' to an audience that will recognise their own homes within the soundworld.

As the sanctity of the home space is cemented; it's role as the space in which a personalised identity can be constructed, free from, and outside of, the overbearing presence of 'the state', so too is it connected to the public realm, or more precisely, its shared affiliation with other similarly constructed home spaces is demonstrated by Porno Para Ricardo in their attempt to bring together a dispersed audience that may never had had the chance to meet in a single place. By highlighting the shared elements of the sound of the home, Porno Para Ricardo construct something of a public homespace; one in which Cubans can express a shared identity, and in which the everyday becomes integral at the point at which the Revolution becomes anachronistic.

Eskuadron Patriota - Who Are 'The People'?: Social Commentary and a Popular Voice

The first concert I ever went to was one with *Grandes ligas,*

Junior Clan, EPG & B. By the end, I was left standing there absolutely hooked...When I got back home from that concert, I was someone else. I don't know what happened, it was something mystical. Something told me: this is what I want to do, from here on out this will be my way to communicate with people. That's when I began my struggle in the world of hip hop. That was in 2000 or 2001. I was twenty-four at that time. (Raudel Collazo Pedroso, aka Escuadrón Patriota, 2011)

Though rock music in all its diverse forms in Cuba is still largely perceived as 'dissident', certain hip-hop musicians have enjoyed something of an official sanction by the state, and the genre has begun to stake a tentative claim at being a recognised 'national' music (Fernandes, 2003, Pacini Hernandez and Garofalo, 1999). However, despite the popularity (and relative acceptance of the genre), many of its more outspoken artists still find themselves subject to strict censorship and marginalisation. One such artist is Raudel Collazo Pedroso - aka Escuadrón Patriota – a musician that, as a consequence of his overtly political lyrics, is forced to a marginal position entirely outside of the state run music industry. He is, as with Porno Para Ricardo, forbidden from performing live in Cuba. Despite this, his music video for the song *'Decadencia'* has become something of an internet sensation since its release in late 2009.

Of the three musicians discussed herein, Escuadrón Partiota is the only one I do not know personally, thus the introductory biography is necessarily scant, relying on secondary sources. I would refer the reader to the Havana Times interview[30] from which one may garner some insight into this remarkable rapper's initiation into, and philosophy regarding, the Cuban rap scene. Suffice to say here it was in this post-millennial moment of reappraisal of the Cuban identity that Raudel was turned onto hip-hop, beginning to make his own music around 2003 (Havana Times, 2011). Raudel is a practising Rastafarian, a fact which further serves to separate him from the state-derived notion of Cuban identity, yet which further asserts his globalised sound and outlook. That he asserts the influence of "Malcolm X, Martin Luther King, Stokely Carmichael, [and] Franz Fanon" (ibid.) on his lyrics, speaks to the *cri de Coeur* social commentary Escaudrón's songs embody. There is also a desire to connect with global political discourses, to express a localised reality with recourse to national cultural elements and a global cultural palette, and to find inspiration in foreign ideas, not to regard them as always already destructive to some obliquely defined 'indigenous' Cuban thinking. The invocation of these four luminaries as influences on Escuadrón's political and cultural map speaks clearly to the desire to fashion a distinctly Black Cuban voice; one capable of expressing the latent, yet still vehement, racism that pervades Cuban society. Yet conversely, as pressing for Escuadrón appears to be the desire to redefine the notion of the 'Cuban people' – *his* people – and foster some sort of shared unity that is not necessarily drawn along racial lines. Particularly the influence of Franz Fanon here speaks of the use of a left wing perspective of subjugation of a group of Cuban society; those not 'within the Revolution'. Escuadrón's lyrics reinvent the definition of what constitutes '*el pueblo*' (the people) by augmenting the identity held within this space, and in doing so, reposition the revolutionary government not as the voice of 'the people', but as the very force oppressing and subjugating them.

"Las Revoluciones Son Para el Pueblo" (Revolutions Are For the People): Leading a New 'Pueblo'

One of the more radical roles assigned to (and occasionally sought by) this counter-hegemonic collection of 'alternative' Cuban musicians is as the voice of the voiceless within Cuba. Gorki Águila has suggested in numerous interviews that one aspect of Porno Para Ricardo's music is to provide an avenue in which the most acerbic thoughts of the population about its leadership can be voiced; a space in which "something that everyone would like to say" (in Cuoma and deNooij, 2008) can be said or felt free from the fear of personal recrimination. In these cases the musician becomes the spokesman, the leader, the voice of the people; social commentary becomes collective affiliation. Certainly this aspect of leadership of the tacit voices of Cuban identity is present within Escuadrón's lyrics in '*Decadencia*':

De nuevo me transformo en la voz de una gran masa
Acéfala, vacía que en silencio se desplaza
Se cansaron de llorar y ahora le sangra el alma
Mientras se preguntan ¿Quién controla su esperanza?
Y se retuercen porque les duele, la herida sangra, y creen que
* mueren*
Quieren gritar su dolor pero no pueden
Porque el terror impuesto le arrancan lo poco que tienen
Piden justicia y eso no se logra ver
¿Por qué reprimen al que libre quiere ser?
Again I become the voice of a great mass
Leaderless, empty, moving in silence
Tired of crying, their souls now bleed
Wondering who controls their hope
And they twist 'cause they hurt, the wound bleeds, they feel
    they're dying
They want to scream their pain, but they can't
Because the imposed terror has got a grab on whatever little
    they have left
They claim justice but it doesn't come through
Why oppressing that who wants to be free?

Escuadrón paints a portrait of contemporary Cuba where '*el pueblo*' – the people – are far from being represented and celebrated by the power structure; indeed they are presented as subjugated, oppressed and voiceless. It is a Cuba in which the revolutionary government censors contesting voices in an attempt to maintain total power; an account not dissimilar to that given by Catherine Moses (see above). But it is into this space of oppression that Escuadrón himself steps; as a leader; a voice to this silent suffering. Paradoxically, it is something of a humble leadership that Escuadrón seems to be assuming; accepted only because of its absolute necessity. He is only *saying* what 'his people' (that is, the community he is a part of, not the community which he is in control of) are *thinking*. Thus his lyrics are given a power of the communal; as if written through and by a collective. It is a incisive, and deeply controversial, redefinition of the Cuban people; one that removed them from the (false) position of equality and representation that the Revolution has claimed on their behalf for over fifty years, and positions them uncomfortably (but perhaps more realistically) as an oppressed *'gran masa'*.

Ye in this redefinition of the Cuban people, the narrative of an oppressed mass and a totalitarian hegemony which must be risen up against is strikingly familiar; it is reminiscent of the type of rhetoric used by the Revolution itself. The pro-revolutionary singer/songrwriter Carlos Puebla paints a similar picture of the Cuban people in the song *'Y en Eso Llego Fidel'* ('And Into This Came Fidel'); an account of the suffering of Cubans at the hand of the overbearing Americans, punctured by the new leader of 'the people' Fidel Castro:

Aquí pensaban seguir, ganando el ciento por cierto
con casas de apartamentos y echar al pueblo a sufrir
y seguir de modo cruel contra el pueblo conspirando
para seguirlo explotando y en esto llegó Fidel.
Y se acabó la diversion, llegó el comandante y mandó a parar
They [the U.S.] thought they could continue, earning 100% with houses and apartments and making the people suffer

and continuing in a cruel way conspiring against the people
to secure their exploitation and into this came Fidel
And now the fun is over, the *commandante* [Fidel Castro]
arrived and ordered them to stop

Though the language of oppression may be similar in both
Puebla's and Escuadrón's accounts of the Cuban people, in the
redefinition of the force acting upon *'el pueblo'* comes a fundamental reassessment of Cuban society. A schism is made apparent
between those truly in power, and those outside it. The revolutionary government – itself once the liberator from oppression -
has warped, claims Escuadrón, over time into the very power it
strove to defeat. It has become the oppressor, and thus has
divorced itself from the 'true people' of Cuba. It is this controversial and potent assertion that is reinforced throughout the first
verse as it builds to a climax. Escuadrón repeatedly reinforces a
unity along class lines rather than espousing the old revolutionary rhetoric of equality along national lines; crucially re-
placing the age-old dividing line of 'them' and 'us' between the
government and the oppressed workers:

Trabajas sudan entero y no te puedes liberar
Entregas todo y a cambio nada, esclavitud total
Así te controlan, yo lo llamo conspiración letal
El mensaje se funde con los segundos, crece mi fe
Inventan leyes abusivas, te tienen a su merced
You work, you sweat your body weight and you can't free
    yourself
You give everything in exchange for nothing, total slavery
This way they control you, I call it lethal conspiracy
The message blends with the seconds, my faith grows
They invent abusive laws, they have you at their mercy

A space of identity is forged, one in which Escuadrón tells his audience of their plight; the hardships of their everyday. By giving voice to these often tacit topics, a new sense of community is constructed, one that is not based around the enforced public displays of fidelity to the Revolution, but around scarcity and oppression. Perhaps it is a space of negative solidarity? One in which, through the recognition of shared endurance, a more realistic (albeit pessimistic) sense of community is forged. This would be true if Escuadrón's rhetoric stopped only at listing the problems of the revolutionary society in modern times, but all this has been building up to a point. This verse, sermon-like, crescendos to a punch line, where Escuadrón delivers the most significant lyric. To accentuate the significance of the line – to reinforce the potency of the message – the backing track cuts away and Escuadrón spits the line with rhythmic passion – and strong Cuban accent - into the microphone:

Nuestras opiniones no se escuchan olvidando
que las revoluciones son para el pueblo,
No para el que esta en el poder
Our opinions are not heard, forgetting
that revolutions are for the people
Not for those in power

The second person 'you' of the retelling of quotidian solidarity is replaced by first person plural – 'our' – a true space of collectivity is defined, and it is one that makes a divide between those in power and *'el pueblo'*; 'the people'. Such an assertion is a radical reclamation of a left-wing identity; one which the Revolution as a socialist endeavour still maintains as its own. Rather like Orwell's pigs in Animal Farm, Escuadrón sees no difference now between the government and previous totalitarian regimes:

Desde sus despachos la realidad no la pueden oler

La tristeza de este país no la van a comprender
They can't smell reality from their offices
The sadness of this country, they can't understand

Of a regime that was built on socialist ideals, to be portrayed as not only removed from the realm of the people, but to be seen as unable to comprehend their plight is a damning indictment. The chorus emphasises the point with a repeated one word castigation: *"Decadencia"* ('Decadence'). The Revolution is portrayed as out of touch; hopelessly inept in defining and unifying *'el pueblo'*; in many ways the antithesis of *'el pueblo'* and their contemporary mores and concerns.

But it is not a just a reactionary lambasting of the Revolution per se, it is more a comment on the longevity of its leaders and the inability to evolve and devolve power to younger generations; it is a generational as much as a political consternation, one that many young Cubans share. The same sort of complaint can be found in Carlos Varela's *'Guillermo Tell'* (see part 2) from twenty years earlier, and yet the issue, for Escuadrón, has yet to have been addressed and is still of paramount importance in shaping the future of Cuba. Many young Cubans today do not feel an opposition to the Revolution as much as they feel a profound disconnection to it; that it was the endeavour of a previous epoch and a previous generation, one which has stifled their opportunity to create their own opinions, and embark upon their own 'revolutions'. The complaint is voiced by Escuadrón in interview:

A revolution was made in Cuba in 1959, not the sole one, but that revolution was made and supposedly it guaranteed all rights to citizens. The Cuban people were eager for that. People never worried a lot about questioning or doubting anything; the people in power made the decisions and no one questioned them. Though there have always been times when people have dared to question, I don't know why I think this current generation is more daring in terms of challenging the established order.

...We weren't directly involved in the revolutionary process. We've been exposed to it, but not concretely. I wasn't at the Bay of Pigs, nor was I around for the Mariel or the Camarioca boatlifts. I wasn't there for the counter-insurgency battles in the Escambray; all that's to say that these weren't events that I experienced. I'm touched by them from a historical point of view...from what I learned in school. Those things were lived through by a different generation, while I've experienced something else, which is what I have to be concerned with. Understand? And since I'm experiencing different phenomena, a different energy, those are the ones I'm trying to confront, to figure out, to question. (Havana Times, 2011)

As with Varela before him, Escuadrón is attempting to usher in a new phase of Cuban history. Such a forthright reappraisal of the Revolution as incapable of voicing the concerns of contemporary Cuban life clears the path for Escuadrón and others to redefine what a truly left-wing imagining of Cuban identity may look like post-millennium. Certainly concepts of rigidly defined boundaries, drawn along geographical and national lines rather than social and cultural ones, are moribund. 'El Pueblo' exists once more in a state of subjugation at the hands of the decadent elite, intent only on consolidating their own power. To resolve this issue, Escuadrón, as with so many young Cubans, looks outside the geographical/ cultural boundaries of his own nation for inspiration. But these disparate sources are always brought to bear on better expressing a contemporary *Cuban* identity, not a desire to 'transcend' nationalism to partake in a globalised melting pot of sounds and styles.

Cultural Connections, Individual Differences

As with both Porno Para Ricardo and Pedro Luis Ferrer (discussed below), there is a drive in Escuadrón's lyrics to expand out geographically and culturally the identity markers permitted as authentic in representing contemporary Cuban identity. In his invocation of the Chilean protest singer Victor Jara[31] (cited as speaking to 'his people' just as Escuadrón speaks to his) and in the prominent display of affiliation to Bob Marley – a banner with Bob Marley's face can be seen above Escuadrón throughout the video, next to a Cuban flag – both point to a reconnection with a pan-Latin American (and pan-Caribbean) culture; links which have been selectively alluded to at best by the Revolution (particularly those with the Caribbean). In light of this pan-national map of cultural influence, Escuadrón appears not only to be cleaving the notion of the Cuban people from its revolutionary government, but also attempting to establish a broader definition of 'the people' that are not constrained by geographical boundaries, but are rather defined by shared experiences of the everyday, history, culture and aspects of identity.

Escuadrón's desire to transcend geographical boundaries push in yet another controversial direction, spanning the ninety mile stretch of water – the Straits of Florida – so often seen as the ineffable boundary line of true Cuban identity to the Revolution. So many Cubans have crossed this boundary – so narrow geographically, so vast politically – in various distinct waves of migration each, again according to Pedraza-Bailey (1985), with its own unique socio-political makeup, each leaving its own trauma on those remaining in Cuba. However, with each passing vintage, the impassability of this ideological-schism-made-geographical, has diminished. Most importantly, the concept that leaving one's Cubanness 'behind' as a prerequisite of migration has been questioned not only by migrants themselves, but by those still living on the island. Certainly those migrants who left during the Special Period have been more reticent to abnegate and excise the

Cubanness from their individual identities, and while much of the work of Cuban migration tends to focus on these condensed 'waves', the post-millennial stream of Cuban migrants who do not necessarily fall into a definite 'vintage', broadly speaking, tend to follow the Special Period trend of maintaining familial and cultural contact with contemporary events in Cuba. As with so much concerning global politics and culture, the internet has served to further shrink the gap – temporally and spatially - between the island and it's emigrant populations (although in Cuba the internet is still a scarce commodity, meaning that access to information from without is still restricted). Increasingly, Cuban identity is seen as existing globally; present in, and defined by, pockets of Cuban residents in numerous places outside the island (Madrid and Miami perhaps most prominently, but also London, New Jersey, Barcelona etc). Yet despite this globalisation, Arturo Arango's assertion that "whatever is Cuban remains a near pathological obsession" (1997:123) is still a pertinent consideration. Despite – or perhaps because of – the prolonged and multi-directional diaspora that has permeated Cuban consciousness, the national is still a principal 'middle ground' between the local and the global, and a central tenet of many personal and collectively constructed identities. Cubanness, for this younger generation, necessarily exists as a global negotiation – if only through the reality of the circumstances that have spread successive generations of Cubans across the world – but it is a negotiation that still seeks to affirm its 'Cubanness'.

Yet in spite of this blurring of national boundaries in contemporary Cuban identity, the Revolution maintains its obsession with the overly-simplistic binary of Havana and Miami – politicised into 'authentically Cuban' and 'gusano'. It is an antiquated rhetoric, one that Escuadrón seeks to critique in the opening lines of the second verse, conflating and incorporating both 'sides' of this obsolete schism back into the definition of the Cuban *'pueblo'*:

Y nos enfrentan, y nos separan en dos bandos
Y vivimos cuidándonos, paranoides, desconfiando
Los mismos hijos del pueblo se están despedazando
Porque el sistema los manipula, y ellos nunca ven el daño
And they put us against each other, and they split up in two
    bands
So we live watching our backs, paranoids, distrusting
The same children of the people tearing each other apart
Because the system manipulates them, and they can't see it

The division into "two bands" speaks of the all-pervading
binarisms around which the revolution (and the many powerful
right-wing groups of Miami-Cubans) have constructed their
visions of Cuban identity. It is not only that these strictly delin-
eated binaries are anathema to generation of Cubans of whom
Escuadrón is a member, but that they are incomprehensible
anachronisms; unable to accurately define the interconnectivity
and global discourse which Cuban from both sides of the
political-geographical divide are engaging with. 'Cuba' exists –
or has been forced to exist – around and through this national
division; 'the people' reside in Miami as they reside in Havana,
they are the "children of the same people" and as such must be
included in the redefinition of what constitutes the Cuban
identity.

Not all of Escuadrón's lyrics promote such blurring of
barriers; such unity. As noted in the section above concerning
Africanness, Blackness and religion, there is also a voice in
Escuadrón's work that insists upon defining the cultural, racial
and social *differences* between members of Cuban society, not to
divide (and illegitimise) certain 'Others'; further fragmenting the
archipelagic individualism of the Special Period, but rather to
give back a distinct voice to the often subjugated Black and

religious voices within Cuba. The line evoking God in a nation still officially atheist points to something of a differentiation between voices:

Dios dame resistencia y toda tu compassion
Solo usted sabe lo que sufre este corazón
God, give me endurance and all your compassion
Only you know what my heart suffers

It is a declamation akin to Pedro Luis Ferrer's invocation of the *Santería* pantheon in *'Amigo Palero'*, where *Yemaya, Changó*, and *Obatalá* are made the truly omnipotent and omniscient forces within Cuba (as opposed to the Revolution and Castro himself), but in Escuadrón's spirituality, there is a recognition and representation of difference, of heterogeneity under a broader rubric of Cubanness. As mentioned, Escuadrón is a practicing Rastafarian, and his musical style, as Sujatha Fernandes eloquently notes in 'Fear of a Black Nation' (2008), evokes something of a demand for a uniquely 'Black' Cuban voice as means of expressing the racial prejudice still experienced by many Black Cubans in the supposedly colourless society. Once more it needs to be asserted that this recognition of difference does not equate to a re-delineation of the boundary of authentic Cubanness as a singular state, outside of which other definitions are positioned as 'inauthentic'. Rather it includes numerous individualised interpretations of cultural symbols within a Cuban framework and is honest in recognising and celebrating the cultural differences which Cubans have.

Ultimately it is an admixture of voices – a true democracy – that Escuadrón is promoting; insisting that the term 'Cuban' is capable of containing a multitude of bespoke opinions, and that only through dialogue between these myriad Cubannesses can a sense of progression – where the constant redefinition of the national identity becomes an on-going and natural process – be achieved:

Y me pregunto si esto es una democracia
¿Por qué pensar diferente es una traición ultranza?
¿Por que a varios sectores se les margina y se les rechaza?
Si no se respeta los criterios, esta nación no avanza
I ask myself if this is a democracy
Why is thinking differently an unforgiveable treason?
Why are some sectors marginalised and rejected?
If different opinions are not respected, the nation won't go
    forward

What is sought by Escuadrón is, above all, a dialogue; one that
incorporates all those who have some vested interest in the term
'Cuban' as a part of their identity. At work in his words is an
almost paradoxical simultaneous bringing together and parti-
tioning of the individualised Cuban voices; those traditionally
divorced from the 'authentic' identity space, and the voicing of
those often subsumed and 'hidden' within it. Once these
composite voices are heard, a new definition of 'the people' can
be considered. It is a discourse of recognising difference, but
demanding a more honest, and constantly negotiated, equality;
something which Escuadrón suggests the revolution has
forgotten about to an extent:

I don't think that free health care and education solves the
problem of a country. There's also individual freedom, and
when I talk about this I'm referring to the individual freedom
of each person to freely express their ideas, to raise them and
defend them openly, even if they go against the established
power... I can't understand how we can build a nation with
one sole opinion, which is also outdated I might add.

It's necessary to think about everybody, because I'm
convinced that my interests aren't the same as those of

someone in their late seventies, and I can't conceive of that person deciding for me. I can't accept it... I think about the question of opportunities, and when I speak to you of opportunities, I'm concerned a great deal about something that has infuriated me for a long time and that's the question of racism in Cuba. (Havana Times, 2011)

Equal access to education and healthcare – the celebrated plus points of the revolutionary government in Cuba – serve to mask what for many Cubans is still a deeply unequal society. Racism, social and cultural prejudice and the single-party political landscape have marginalised many personal freedoms within Cuba; and worse have submerged them in a society that purports to champion equality. Perhaps this is where Castro's mantra "within the revolution; everything" is at its most dangerous. When a political movement is made synonymous with nation and national identity (Moses, 2000), what is left out of the revolutionary narrative, yet still exists within the country, is sidelined, and made voiceless. Escuadrón's lyrics attempt to give voice to these subjugated aspects of Cuban identity by redrawing the boundary lines of Cuban identity and reconnecting 'el pueblo' across nations along social and cultural affiliations. His is a cry for differentiation, but equality among those social, cultural and racial differences. For Escuadrón, 'el pueblo' is pan-national – drawn and defined by culture and class, not by always already existent nationalism. Cuban identity must contain conversation, constant negotiation and redefinition, and must include all its disparate voices, not under separated banners and subcultures, but under one same complex national identity.

Pedro Luis Ferrer - Changüi Para la Pena: Reconnecting Cuba Temporally and Spatially

I am my own version of *Cubanía*, and I refuse to let myself by trampled by the dictates of the past or of tradition. I think that all attempts at rancid nationalism are dangerous. Tradition offers us effective resources for communication, with its arsenal of common codes and signs, but a repetition of tradition tends to bore and tire society. Cultures need to conserve themselves by constant renovation, which is my objective in making music. (Pedro Luis Ferrer, in Navarro, 2005)

Pedro Luis Ferrer's career in music is almost as long and as chequered as the Revolution itself. Ferrer is a singer/songwriter who grew up with Cuban rural music, yet came of age as rock music began to seep into the island. Along with many of his contemporaries, he was similarly inspired by the protest songs and various folk revivals both of Latin America and the U.S.; the result was a movement called *nueva trova;* in which the *cantautor* (singer/songwriter) became a social commentator, utilising poetic, allegorical and often humorous lyrics to convey their message. Ferrer's early songs became immensely popular in Cuba, and his place within the pantheon of 'Cuban Greats' seemed assured. However, as his social commentaries became less humorous, and the allegory scarcely opaque, the hand of state oppression began to bear down upon him. Deemed 'too controversial', there followed an almost total censorship of his music from radio and television in the late 1980s and early 1990s[32]. At no time was the exact cause of the censorship explained to Ferrer, but nonetheless he became one of the many musicians forced to exist in a non-position "outside the Revolution".

The new millennium has seen Ferrer undergo something of a renaissance, expanding his body of work significantly by releasing three self-recorded albums; *'Rústico'* (2005) and *'Natural'* (2006) on Escondida Records, and *'Tangible'* (2010) on Ultra Records. While this most recent album returns to a fuller soundscape – trumpets, piano, and timbales are all visitors once more – Ferrer entered the lucrative world music market with his paired down *'bunga'*[33] consisting of Ferrer himself occasionally on guitar, but most notable playing the *trés*, Lerlys Morales (guitar) and Lena Ferrer (percussion) providing lush harmonies and Basilio Perodín completing the line-up, providing a cavalcade of percussion, including the *marímbula*.[34] Though until recently[35] Ferrer was still not permitted to perform live in Cuba, his position in the Cuban music scene is certainly less clear cut than Escuadrón Patriota or Porno Para Ricardo. He now exists in a confusing, liminal space between censorship and acceptance. Though he seems to deliberately eschew publicity and attention within Cuba, and is certainly not venerated by the Revolution, he has managed, in this past decade, to travel and perform outside of Cuba with relative regularity, and to rekindle the respect and popularity of a truly accomplished musician within Cuba.

Musically, Ferrer has championed more elusive and less celebrated forms of Cuban music – notable *changüi*, a style of music native to the easternmost province of *Guantánamo* – documenting these forgotten moments of Cuban history to paint a more vibrant portrait of the island's cultural heritage. However, alongside the will to preserve is the necessity to reinvent, and so Ferrer melds and moulds these traditions into a vehicle capable of expressing social commentary that looks forward and back simultaneously, bridging the often cleaved epochs of Cuba's history. His albums combine 'traditional' Cuban musical elements with contemporary inventions; biting, yet poetic and allegorical social commentary. Significantly, Ferrer attempts not only to connect contemporary Cuba temporally, but also spatially, by presenting and a pan-Latin American and pan-Caribbean scope that locates Cuba within a broader cultural, political and social climate. The aim is to dispel the myth of global isolation and autochthonous cultural (and thus political) production within the island. Ferrer aims to connect the cultural, historical and social mores of Cuba into more globalised discourses, and to recognise that such links have always been crucial in defining a Cuban identity. In illuminating these spatial and temporal links, Ferrer attests to the fact that the Cuban nation, and identity, are subject to change and that the rigidified (politically motivated) unison of the Cuban identity is at best a partial definition, and at worst woefully inadequate for representing a vibrant, diverse nation that is re-establishing its position within the global society.

Rewriting the Map: A Spatial Connection

As has been alluded to throughout this work, a tendency exists within Cuban discourse to portray Cuban music as 'unique'; a culture formed in an isolated crucible that is not only distinguishable from its neighbouring countries, but can also be unintelligible to them. As Raúl Fernandez suggests of Cuban music:

> People of Latin American origin can be nearly as unfamiliar with Spanish-Caribbean music as US-Anglo audiences... the *clave* beat, the rhythmic use of 'melody' instruments, and a melodic approach to percussion produce exotic sounds even for many Latin Americans. (1994:111)

The political motivations of such a rhetoric are self-evident. By asserting a cultural difference between Cuba and even its closest neighbours, a political and social schism is forged; one where no influence from without can be permitted, where "Cuba, the *patria* (fatherland), has been linked to socialism, and socialism to Fidel" (Moses, 2000:24), and thus anything coming from outside of that narrow space is unable to take even a constituent place in defining Cuban identity.

Although examples of the melding of rhythm and melody propounded by Fernandez can be found within Ferrer's work - the polyrhythmic, yet distinctly melodic percussion in tracks

76

such as 'La Tarde Se Ha Puesto Triste' and 'Anana Oye', or the rhythmic, percussive picking of the trés on tracks such as 'Taitaíto'[36] – the context within which Ferrer utilises these musical devices makes them anything but an exclusive (or exclusivist) trope comprehendible only to Cubans. Ferrer is keen to place his musical traditions within a global context; to explain them to and draw parallels with cultural practices from other countries, particularly those from Latin America and the Caribbean:

> I try to say two things to the audiences I work with. One, that I work with traditions – with what I would like traditions to be and with my imagination most of all to make music that is somehow still Cuban but is, at the same time, universal and at the same time that contributes new things to those existing traditions. In that way, I try to be as free as I can. I think the European audiences – which are the audiences I have worked with the most in the last few years - understand this and they assimilate it very well, they enjoy it a lot. (Ferrer, 2010)

There is more than just a necessity to appeal to the ever-expanding (and ever-lucrative) 'world music' marketplace here, though that, for a musician unable to ply his trade freely within Cuba, is undeniably important. Perhaps Ferrer is attempting to demystify Cuban musical tropes, or even just to present them to an audience within a more natural context of tradition and innovation by re-connecting Cuba geographically to a broader cultural network. One overt way in which Ferrer locates Cuban 'uniqueness' is by developing a cultural map of flow and exchange As an example, in the song 'Changüí Para La Pena' ('Changüí For Sadness'), Ferrer makes reference to a number of significant places:

Haití se encuentra cerca. Jamaica está en la esquina.

A un paso Puerto Rico. Changüi.
Guantánamo, La Sierra. La Habana, mi Changüisa[37]
Haiti is near, Jamaica is around the corner.
A step away is Puerto Rico. Changüi.
Guantanamo, La Sierra, Havana, my Changüisa

This verse plays out something of a journey around the Caribbean, picking up influences, moving through Cuba and ending with Ferrer's contemporary interpretation: *'my Changüisa'*. Everything is 'just around the corner'; everything within touching distance. Not only does this condensation of physical space reinforce the connectedness of Cuba to the rest of the Caribbean, it further serves to legitimise the use and incorporation of cultural influence from these nations into a renewed sense of culturally connected Cubanness. Further accentuating the contemporaneousness of cultural flow, Ferrer bookends the list of Cuban place names mentioned not with the 'traditional' *Changüi*, but with his 'own' genre; *Changüisa*. The formation of Cuban identity is made an on-going process in Ferrer's cultural map. In the assertion of a new form – *Changüisa* – Ferrer is charged with the role of the contemporising tradition, of bringing it into its modern form, but in doing so, one has to recognise the flows of information that permeate modern Cuba. In his cultural map of the Caribbean is an assertion that Cuban identity can absorb influences from without, can change itself over time, without losing its essential 'Cubanness'.

As well as demonstrating the cultural connections with the Caribbean, Ferrer also asserts a pan-Americanism, sketching out a historical/cultural map of interconnectivity between Cuba and its neighbours. In the song *'¿Cómo Viviré, Mi Cholita?'* ('How Will I Live, My *Cholita?'*)[38], Ferrer makes a more pointed political reference. Ostensibly portraying the plight of an Andean coca farmer, the pressures of government (and U.S.) intervention, and the prohibitions strangling innovation, *'Como Viviré...'* blurs the boundaries between a Latin American and a Cuban reality. The titular *Cholita*, a term used in the Andes and not in Cuba, along with the use of the *cajón* – a percussion instrument associated most notably with Afro-Peruvian music – would tend to place this song as a tableau of life outside of Cuba; perhaps even a commentary on the advantageous position Cuba finds itself, removed from the dominance of the 'Colossus to the North'. Yet that most ubiquitous of Cuban markers – the heartbeat *clavé* – anchors the song back in Cuba; the story of the coca farmer is transposed over a Cuban rhythm; *cholita* becomes *mamita*! The use of the *cajón* (also called the Peruvian box) within an otherwise Cuban soundworld created something of its own minor controversy outside of the lyrical content of this song, as this except from the press release shows:

> The Peruvian box has a sympathetic sound with the guitar and better capacity for subtleties—it has a hole in the back giving it more tonality and a loose plank that creates a snare-like sound; whereas the Cuban version is closed and sturdy. That doesn't mean I won't use the *rumba* box one day. (Ferrer, 2002, *Rústico* press release)[39]

Whether this somewhat apologetic justification of organological hybridity is aimed at appeasing world music aficionados searching for 'authentic Cuban tradition', or whether it alludes to a desire to foster an overtly pan-American soundscape is perhaps a moot point. But it does accentuate Ferrer's insistence on selection and opening up the possibilities of what can be considered part of a Cuban soundscape, further demonstrating that, when necessary, it is possible to search outside of Cuba for ingredients to best express an individual sentiment. Ferrer is by no means confined by the narrow definition of what constitutes an authentic expression of Cuban identity, yet by the same token, whatever he incorporates into his message, he does so to better –

that is more accurately - express his message *as a Cuban*. There is not a rejection of Cubanness here, rather an attempt to expand the paradigm out to include yet more influences; to reintroduce a fluidity and malleability into the rigidity of revolutionary rhetoric.

Lyrically, '*¿Cómo Viviré, Mi Cholita?*' operates on the same thinly-veiled allegorical platform as *'Guillermo Tell'* by Carlos Varela, and numerous other songs by Ferrer himself. Rather than being (just) a tableau of an exotic other, Ferrer is using the plight of the Andean farmer to express the similarities in the Cuban situation:

Se permite el hambre, la espera
permitido el miedo, la ausencia; se prohíbe amar...
Que si no vendo cosas prohibidas, como viviré?
Que el poder prohíbe y prohíbe, como viviré?
Ay, que el dinero nunca me alcanza, no, como viviré?
Que por mi esfuerzo nada me pagan, como viviré?...
Que no me digan siempre lo mismo, como viviré?
Hunger and waiting are allowed,
fear and absence are permitted; love is prohibited...
If I don't sell illegal things, how will I live?
If the powers prohibit and prohibit, how will I live?
If the money they pay me is not enough, how will I live?
If no one pays me for my effort, how will I live?...
Don't always tell me the same thing, how will I live?

Ferrer is talking about the Andes, but he is simultaneously refer-encing the plight in Cuba, where many of the same concerns abound – the reliance on black markets, an overly zealous political rhetoric, a constant feeling of waiting, a vast discrepancy between those paid in *pesos convertibles,* the monetary system that mirrors the price of the US Dollar, and those paid in *peso cubanos* (as most Cubans are), and, above all, an anger at the recalcitrance of the government to prohibiting Cubans to adapt and thrive in the everyday by strictly monitoring all activity. Once again, Ferrer is highlighting the similarities between Cuba and its (Latin) American neighbours, rather than portraying Cuban culture as somehow separate and 'hard to understand' for those coming from 'outside', and this desire to emphasise the similarities in the plight of Cubans and Latin Americans serves the purpose of reconnecting Cuba in a more pragmatic and realistic way with its Latin-American neighbours, dispelling the myth of Cuba as the 'ideal state', as it is often romanticised by Latin Americans (and many Europeans) as well as by the Revolution itself. By recognising the shared problems that exist in Cuban and Latin American societies – disparity of wealth, political censorship and economic hardship – Ferrer seeks not to distance himself from a Cuban identity, but rather to bring it into a wider fold, to seek a realism behind the veil of false utopianism of the Revolution.

But in doing so, I don't think Ferrer rejects the Revolution, or its utopianism, out of hand. Rather, his aim is to lament rather than to lambast. The source of his frustration is with the bureaucracy and stagnation of the revolution which has left it out of touch with 'the people'. In much the same way as Escuadrón Patriota does (though with less acerbity, and more of a world-weary regret) Ferrer talks of the Revolution, the veil of allegory removed, in the quite beautiful song 'Yo no Tanto Como El':

Detesto la burocracia que convirtió eficacia
En un montón de desgracias. De vanas prohibiciones
Aumentaron los rencores y mataron mil amores
Qué ha pasado con la vida
tanta gente arrepentida?
I detest the bureaucracy that converted efficacy
into a mountain of misfortune. Of vain prohibitions
That augmented grudges And killed one thousand loves

What has happened to life for so many to repent?

As with Escuadrón's reclamation of the notion of 'the people' from the revolution, Ferrer forges a new definition of the people, alluding here to Cubans who have left Cuba, their grudges augmented to the point of insupportability. But crucially he references the once-efficient regime that, though a lack of ability (or willingness) to change and redefine itself, has become obsolete in defining the Cuban nation. As a result, Ferrer finds common ground in Latin American and the Caribbean, and attempts to bridge gaps between Cuban and other traditions, looking both for those cultural forms outside of Cuba with which he feels a personal, aesthetic connection, irrespective of a link with the narrow definition of Cuban tradition and identity outlined by the Revolution.

Re-Presenting Tradition: A Temporal Connection, A Modern Approach

It is not only spatially throughout the continent, but temporally through Cuba's fractious and fractured history, that Ferrer seeks to re-establish connections in painting a more representative portrait of Cuban identity. In the compartmentalisation of Cuban history into evental epochs, binarisms of 'before and after', 'inside and outside', 'authentic and inauthentic' pervade so much of Cuban discourse. As a result, there is often a disavowal of the 'epoch that came before'. Such a disavowal can be seen in the Revolution's attitude to Platt Amendment Cuba, but then again, the nostalgic representations of Cuba of the Buena Vista Social Club perhaps show a similar negation of the revolutionary epoch by harking (exclusively) back to pre-revolutionary styles and recording techniques (cf. Perna, 2005:240 and Barker and Taylor, 2007:297). While one could scarcely contest the evental nature of both the Special Period and Revolution, and the need to construct a "new way of being" (Badiou, 2001:42) in their wake, such redefinitions often tend to leave out the still-present remnants of the previous epoch. Fragments of identity, styles of music, art, culture, social symbols and ways of being are lost in the cracks of these slabs of history; those who feel some connection to these lost symbols are either subjugated – forced to either keep these parts of their identity hidden, or relinquish them - or else they are disallowed from the newly constructed identity. Part of what Ferrer's music seeks to do is mine these chasms and lost faces of Cubanness, bringing them 'back' to the present as a method of reconnecting the schisms in the nation's history. In doing so, the singularity of Cubanness is inevitably problematised, as a historical authenticity is afforded to these 'forgotten' genres of music. Because his theorisation on his own music making is so eloquent, I recount here Ferrer's own words at length:

[I want] to experiment with these ideas, from taking on seeds of Cuban music genres that I have found throughout the island, seeds that are either forgotten or not given importance, and I take them to another dimension and try to make a music that may at times not even seem Cuban, but I have knowledge that it is part of our culture. My problem is that I don't have a musicological sense of music. I don't feel like a scientist, I just feel like an artist. So whilst a scientist tries to find an objective truth outside of his feelings, I, as an artist, do the opposite. For me, the truth is found in the artistic work that I do and the success of my thesis is in my artwork. I sometimes try to fill in gaps that musicology doesn't fill in for me. So I speculate a lot. I have my own speculations and what I cannot find through scientific investigation, I invent it and recreate it. So, that's why I speak about some sort of artistic historicity. My vision is not as musicological, although I do work based on some musicological work, but this sometimes seems insufficient to me. I also take from what I find around, from my daily experience of my life in Cuba, so I work with that and I create my artwork, and in the process, I also find musics from other countries that share those seeds. In the end, we are a new country, a country that is still being made, even though it already has *'chachacha'*, *'son'* and *'mambo'*, we still are a new born culture and we will continue growing, and many things will continue being Cuban in history but, for example, you cannot say that *danzón*[40] is the national dance when nobody dances *danzón*.

I have a good relationship with tradition, but with some distance and detachment because I don't think tradition has to behave like a dictatorship over what I have to do in the present. I also have the right to speculate and imagine things. I have found many seeds throughout the island that take me to cultures that came from abroad. Because in the end this is a country made with men that came from other continents, from millenary cultures. So in that sense I feel that by taking on tradition I am relating more and more with the world. Not only to I intend to experiment with those elements that I find here, but also with others that I find I am in tune with in other cultures, simply because I enjoy them. Sindo Garay,[41] for example, wrote his music under the influx of Italian opera which was very popular in Cuba at the time. Take one of Sindo's songs, such as *'Perla Marina'*, and you sing it in Italian, and it feels like it was an Italian song. So, he drank from those fountains which were of his time, which moved him and he re-elaborated them to make the songs he made, which are amazing... But again, he took influence from the world. So why if a man like Sindo was capable of taking from the world around him, why don't I have the same rights?...

I think that going deeper into and exploring traditions one can also free oneself of dogma that is born out of the institutionalisation of tradition. There are certain dogmas when people start saying 'this is like this', same as with stereotypes, when we say 'Cubans are like this, Cubans are like that,

Cubans are happy' but Cubans are different in so many ways. Cubans are like Ñico Saquito but also like Jose Martí[42] who never ever laughed. [laugh]. Yeah! Can you think of anything funny that Marti ever wrote in his books? But he's Cuban as well! In music I simply use elements that are in tune with me, same as with food. Some people like cod, some people like rice, some like beans. Not all Cubans like black beans or pork. So, within this that makes us Cuban, each person chooses what each person likes or finds himself in tune with according to their sensibility. The music I make is, to a large extent, an abstraction of the cultural reality that surrounds me. That's how I see it...

The issue here is that in the world, there is also a preconceived perception of what Cuba is due to commerce – what is commercialised, not only through the Buena Vista Social Club, but also even before the revolution, the companies that traded or exploited Cuban music throughout the world were giving an image of what Cuba was. With the boom of *chachacha* and *mumbo* etcetera. So there is a preconceived image of what Cuban music is. Later on, with *nueva trova* as well, with *'filin'*.[43] All these genres and elements integrated into what became the image – the photograph – of what Cuban music is and that has an impact – a weight. When people see me performing, people notice that I approximate that tradition of what Cuban music is, but that I am also step outside of it. So I explain this, and people find it very attractive because also people are bored of the same thing. At least in the stages where I have performed... you find an audience that is very interested in discovering new music from Cuba. They show interest when I tell them about *changüi*. I even tell them that my music is not representative of what traditional *changüi* is, because I don't do *'coro de clave'*.[44] I take *changüi* into account to create music, because my creation comes from there – *changüi* is not something that

I made up. I feel that people see me as someone who is close to that fixed image of what Cuban music is, but also as someone who detaches themselves from it and can step out of it. And also someone who sometimes has nothing to do with that image at all [laugh]. So I find this very interesting.

Sometimes I speak about traditions that are unknown within Cuba; local traditions... things I used to see in *Yaguajay*[45] when I was a child, I never imagined they would be of any use. Then one day I realised I could do something with them and so you start working with them – they are experiments. Sometimes reconstructing things that you keep safe in your imagination, things that aren't exactly as you think they are. Because these are things that happened a long time ago, they are fragments of my childhood, so you don't remember them very well, but they are still in your mind. I saw them, I give them a name and I say that these things are part of a tradition, which is true – I saw them there, I didn't invent them – but if you go there [*Yaguajay*] now, they don't exist anymore. Maybe someone remembers that in the neighbourhood '*sansaria*' that those *Sones* used to be played. But they come across as more of a circumstantial experience of the time because although many towns do generate traditions that are artistic in essence, if they are not commercialised or documented – written down – they disappear. If there is not an artist that recreates them, they disappear. So that's what I do. And I perceive that the audience I relate to knows this, because I tell them as well. Not only do I tell my audience about existing known traditions, but I'm also telling them about things that were traditional in the past and have disappeared – that are almost non-existent. I was lucky to have lived and seen a lot of these lost traditions in *Yaguajay* thus I have seen in Cuba things that have been circumstantial that afterwards I have gone to find out more about them and they have vanished. That's why I believe so much in the importance of the artist as a creator or re-creator of these almost lost traditions. As he somehow documents them, albeit from his own, personal vision. *Changüi*, for example, has been developed a bit more as a dance, but little has been done with it when it comes to song. (Ferrer, 2010)

Ferrer sees no problem in taking influence from anywhere he chooses, because it is an individual conception of Cubanness that he is constructing. There is a move away from the old definitions of a socialist Cuban identity - the single, national voice - but an approach towards a more social Cubanness that is constructed from a spectrum of individual Cubannesses that blend together in the public space, and thus have the capability to house multiple forms and myriad variations. It is a more holistic, and much more robust Cuban identity that Ferrer espouses, one that may borrow from both his own country's stable of 'traditional' music, but also coterminous forms from outside.

But Ferrer's multifaceted Cubanness is not only a rebuttal of revolutionary rhetoric, it is also aimed at the globalisational view of the local which attempts to pare down each nation into a recognisable, synecdochical form; easily comprehended and fitted into a broad narrative. Ferrer reasserts a kind of middle ground – that of the nation – back into the local/global discourse; a space of cultural complexity, yet of specificity; a space in which global and local cultural sources are melded to represent and reflect a shared experience of place and time. By adopting, adapting, and ultimately contemporising genres such as *changüi*, Ferrer is reclaiming a disvalued (within the realm of 'official' discourse) branch of Cuban music, and by celebrating it, is both making it contemporary and providing insight into the difference within Cuba's traditional past. One must be wary here of painting Ferrer as some sort of folk music 'collector'; lamenting the lost traditions of his nation and attempting to 'revive' them. This is not Ferrer's aim in the slightest. He is quick to note that traditions can only be considered relevant if they speak to a contemporary reality. Concepts such as 'revival' and 'preservation' of that which has been lost are not on Ferrer's agenda; rather a sense of renovation and reclamation of that which has been left out.

Conclusion: Towards the Future of Cuban Music Making

> Those who have spent their lifetimes studying Cuba know that predicting its future has always been a fool's errand. (Lisandro Pérez, 2008:85)

With Pérez's sagely words resounding, the conclusion to this short work is necessarily less than conclusive, for what may be said of the future of Cuban music making, when the present appears so precarious? Cuba finds itself on something of a perennial tipping point; one always threatening to tip the island into a(nother) new epoch. But as with so many potential evental moments in Cuba's post-revolutionary history – the missile crisis, the collapse of the Soviet Union, the mass waves of migration, the relinquishing of power by Fidel Castro – somehow, a degree of continuity – the Revolution itself – is maintained. And importantly, for many young Cubans both inside and outside the island, the insistence is still to define a *Cuban* identity, rather than embrace a global, nationless identity. Antoni Kapcia has written of the necessary recourse to continuity in discussing Cuba's history:

> To talk of continuity, in the context of an apparently ever-changing Revolution, is inevitably to invite surprise among lay observers, used to seeing the process portrayed as a zigzag trajectory... the 'history by phases' approach has also been tempting because it becomes easier to explain the contradictions that have characterized the whole process by categorising periods, hegemonies and directions. (2000:221)

Though parsed into epochs by many (this work included), Cuban identity is one of continuity, history and gradual change. So waiting on the final eventual signifier – the death of Fidel Castro – for some grand change to occur would perhaps appear to be waiting in vain.

As the work of these three musicians – representational of a broad gamut of contemporary Cuban music makers – would attest, there is a necessity not to entirely redefine a Cuban identity, but to *better* define it; that is, not to 'territorialise', or 'reterritorialise' the identity space of Cubanness, to use that well-worn Deleuzian terminology – destroying old definitions and building new ones in their place – but perhaps to cohabit that space of identity; to augment it, to problematise it and recontextualise it, to allow multiple nuanced definitions to be held under one same rubric: Cubanness. Neither is it a homogenous, singular identity space, nor a fragmented and individualistic archipelago; rather a truly radical 'Thirdspace' – an Aleph – in which *difference* is celebrated, and thus made *equal*.

Rather than grand, epochal change, perhaps what these musicians represent is a gradual, and thus manageable, change that is self-determined and representational of *'el pueblo'*. Fundamentally, this demands a reclamation of the left-wing, away from a revolutionary government which, through the ravages of over fifty years of obstinately maintained power, and often brutal censorship, have distanced themselves from truly socialist ideals of giving power to the masses. Through modest campaigns to reclaim the means of cultural production, by recognising diversity, yet reforging a unified Cuban identity, and in the noble attempt to speak *of* and *for* the people; to say what they daren't – in short, by working outside the Revolution – these musicians restate and reclaim a left-wing that is democratic, representational and forward-facing. A significant, yet subtle change appears, but it is one that maintains a continuity.

There is no doubt that Cuba is changing – politically, socially and economically – and that previously held notions of isolation from globalisation are all but moribund to even the most staunch revolutionary. These changes have been slow and frustrating, and often only legitimise what has been happening surreptitiously anyway. The most recent acquiescence is that Cubans are now able to buy and sell houses, rather than the convoluted process of 'swapping' houses. Yet in part, the reticence to change comes from the pervasive fear – real or imagined – of U.S. dominance, and this is a fear held not only by the government, but by many Cubans themselves. The notion of becoming a U.S. Commonwealth (as Puerto Rico) is anathema to most Cubans, not only politically, but in socio-cultural terms as well. The nation and national identity are still proud identity markers for many Cubans, even those opposed to the Revolution itself. The homogenisation of Cuban music, culture and identity into a globalised recapitulation of American genres and styles is a fear of many Cubans, and one played out in many nations around the world. But as I hope to have presented in these brief case studies, and as many working on contemporary Cuban music have noted (see particularly Pacini Hernandez et al. 2004), the adoption and adaption of 'foreign' musics does not necessarily represent a step closer to global homogeneity, nor does it suggest an insidious forcing of U.S. culture usurping 'tradition' and wiping the indigenous from the map. The punk of Porno Para Ricardo, the hip hop of Escuadrón and the *Changuisa* of Pedro Luis Ferrer, are as distinctly Cuban as rumba or mambo, and as culturally varied from their American counterparts as are these ostensibly 'indigenous' genres. What this generation of diverse sounding Cuban musicians represent is the ability to choose from a more global palette of influences, but these genres, styles and sounds will always be utilised to represent a *Cuban* identity, and will thus always have about them a unique flavour that speaks to and of *Cubanía*. The future musicians of Cuba will, there is no doubt, be as idiosyncratic, as talented, and as unmistakably Cuban, as their much celebrated forbears.

And so, in a nation that has lived for so long contesting the boundary between two oppositional and finite binaries, what is most important is the recognition that these two oppositional 'sides' of the argument are not only undesirable, but are anachronistic. The choice is no longer between a socialist yet totalitarian revolution and either exile or protectorship from a right-wing United States. What is being sought is a much broader wealth of intermediate voices, and that these voices are incorporated into a singular, albeit complex, Cuban identity.

The future of Cuban music making will be, as it always has been, a reflection of the future of Cuban society. It will continue to diversify, celebrating different influence and opinion, whilst always maintaining a keen sense of the local, via recourse to a shared wealth of tradition, cultural signifiers and history.

Notes

1. The exact date(s) of the Special Period are hard to pin down. In many ways, their effects are still palpable within Cuba today. Broadly speaking, the years 1989- 1995 represented the most traumatic of the Special Period.

2. Fernando Ortiz makes the salient point that "since the sixteenth century all classes, races, and cultures, coming in [to Cuba] by will or by force, have all been exogenous and have all been torn from their places of origin, suffering the shock of this first uprooting and a harsh trans- planting"(1995:100). This coupled with the near-total extinction of the indigenous population has perhaps increased the necessity (and the ability) to imagine what constitutes the 'indigenous culture' of the island.

3. The *clavé* rhythm is the central rhythmic structure utilised in many of Cuba's most synonymous musical forms – particu- larly *son* and *rumba* – it is most often played using *clavés* (wooden poles which produce a high-pitched tone) and reads, in western notation, as either a 2 beat-3 beat, or vice versa, a pattern played over two bars of 4/4.

4. The images Perez is talking about here are those of sexualised, hedonistic dance music, which "respectable Cuban society" baulked at (Perez, 1999:202).

5. The use of the verb '*Tener*' (to have), is not so remarkable in Spanish, as it is used often where in English the verb 'to be' would be used (e.g. when discussing age, emotional state etc). However, this literal English translation as 'to *have* from a place' does throw up some interesting ruminations about ownership of history and characteristics of identity.

6. Another telling connection to Africa which exists outside these 'finished root' paradigms is the Cuban operations in the Angolan civil war of the 1970s.

7. For examples of Cuba's political billboards, see the following websites: http://news.bbc.co.uk/1/hi/in_depth/7805963.stm, http://www.flickr.com/photos/stml/sets/72157604396971546/ and http://www.havanatimes.org/?p=28725

8. "The words Cuba and Havana are synonymous with the delights, the virtues, and the vices of the smoker. We all know that the luxury, the enjoyment, the aesthetics, and the snobbishness of smoking tobacco are associated with these three syllables: Havana." (Bronislaw Malinowski, 1995:lxi)

9. One common billboard slogan is that of revolutionary commander Camilo Cienfuegos: *"vas bien, Fidel"* ("you're doing fine, Fidel").

10. During George W. Bush's tenure in the White House, billboards likening him to Hitler were not an uncommon theme.

11. The word *'gusano'* literally translates into English as 'worm'. It is the pejorative epithet given to 'traitors' to the revolution, and is most commonly used to refer to those Cubans who emigrated to Miami.

12. Piotr Sztompka's term "traumatogenic change" is defined with recourse to four broad traits:

    The traumatogenic change seems to exhibit four traits. First, it is characterised by specific speed. The obvious case is that the change is *sudden* and *rapid*, occurring within a span of time relatively short for a given kind of process... The second trait of traumatogenic change has to do with its scope. It is usually *wide, comprehensive,* either in that it touches many aspects of life – be it social or personal life – or that it affects many actors and many actions...

    Third, traumatogenic change is marked by specific context, particularly substance, either in the sense that it is *radical, deep, fundamental* – that is, it touches the core aspects of social life or personal fate – or that it affects universal experience...

The fourth feature... has to do with the specific mental frame with which it is encountered by the people. It is faced with an *unbelieving mood*; it is at least to some extent unexpected, surprising, precisely "shocking" in the literal sense of the word (2004:158-9).

Though the complexities and traumatic personal (and national) moments that constituted this most difficult of periods in Cuba would warrant a much larger analysis that this book can offer, I believe that Sztompka's four-part definition broadly defines the experience of many Cubans during the Special Period.

13. *Timba* is a genre of Cuban music, with its roots firmly in *salsa* that became popular in the 1980s and 90s. For a detailed account of this fascinating genre, see Vincenzo Perna's book, '*Timba: The Sound of the Cuban Crisis*' (2005).

14. It is interesting to note that this live version of the song, rather than the album recording, appears on Varela's 'best of' album '*Los Hijos de Guillermo Tell*' (The Children of William Tell) and on the Luaka Bop compilation '*Diablo al Infierno!*'.

15. This amendment allowing Cubans to stay in tourist hotels was passed in 2008 by Raul Castro. The details (albeit from a partisan perspective) of this amendment can be found at the following website. www.msnbc.com/id/23878991.

16. I must pay a debt of gratitude to my wife – a Cuban musician who worked in a tourist hotel, and studied English at University during the Special Period - for this account of tourist-student interaction.

17. Though, as will be discussed below, Pedro Luis Ferrer has been performing since the mid-1960s, the new millennium has seen something of a rebirth of his musical career, releasing three albums since the mid-2000s.

18. The word *friki* is a Spanish rendering of the English word 'freaky'. In Cuba it is used as a catch all phrase for

participants in Cuba's alternative music scenes (predominantly rockers, goths, punks, etc. – such as these terms are applicable to Cuba.)

19. The *trés* is a six stringed cousin of the guitar, native to Cuba. The strings are arranged in three courses of two strings, and commonly tuned G-C-E.

20. This assertion is taken from an interview (MLC, 2008) in which Gorki asserts: "a lot of people [in Cuba] want to hear what we say in out lyrics since that is what many people think but are incapable of expressing because of fear."

21. The title of this record is somewhat difficult to translate, owing to the double meaning of the word *'masas'* – 'masses' and 'meat' in English. Thus the album title is something like 'Rock for the Masses/Meat... Carnivores'

22. Videos of their typically subversive performances can be found here: http://www.youtube.com/watch?v=W4Uk5gs Hlas. Gorki is here parodying the singing style of Silvio Rodriguez.

23. *Pinar del Rio* is the most westerly province in Cuba.

24. A large number of articles detailing the events of Gorki's incarceration, and several more detailing further examples of his involvements with the Cuban authorities are archived here: http://www.freemuse.org/sw1534.asp

25. Gorki speaks of his time in prison in the documentary 'Cuba Rebelión' (Cuomo and de Nooij, 2009).

26. The AHS is a government-funded agency to which musicians must belong to be afforded rehearsal space, concerts and any sense of legitimacy within Cuba's tightly controlled music 'industry' (Garcia-Freyre, 2008:556).

27. "I am Porno, I am Popular", "I don't like politics, but she likes me" and "The Red Album".

28. The band also released an EP containing selected tracks from their first album with Mexican record label *Discos Antídotos*. This EP is only available in Mexico.

29. The phrase *"seremos como el Che"* – "we will be like Che" – is one maxim of quasi-religious proportions that the revolution has founded its concept of Cuban identity upon. It is written on countless murals and billboards throughout the country, and repeated by schoolchildren and *pioneros* daily.

30. Found here: http://www.havanatimes.org/?p=37846

31. The lyric comes at the end of the chorus: *"Como Víctor Jara diciéndole a su pueblo la libertad esta cerca"* ("like Víctor Jara telling his people, freedom is near").

32. During this period of censorship, Pedro Luis Ferrer suffered some personal recrimination from the government. I have been unable to find any information on this subject, and felt unable to ask about it in interview. I believe, from hints Ferrer has given to mutual friends, that he was sent to some sort of work camp for dissident artists.

33. *'Bunga'* is a Cuban word that means a small, informal group of musicians.

34. The *marímbula* is a large boxlike thumb piano and was a progenitor of the Double Bass in much of Cuba's rural music.

35. See: http://www.havanatimes.org/?p=46253

36. Track 4 on *'Pedro Luis Ferrer'*, and tracks 9 and 3 on *'Natural'* respectively

37. Guantanamo is the Eastern most province of Cuba, and the 'birth place' of *Changüi*. *'La Sierra'* means 'the mountains' and could refer to *'Sierra Maestra'* in the East of Cuba. *Changüisa* is the name Ferrer gives to his own modern take on the traditional genre.

38. The term *'cholita'* is somewhat difficult to translate into English, particularly given its relocated meaning in the work of Pedro Luis Ferrer. In its Andean context, it refers to someone of Amerindian ancestry. Though throughout the Americas it has often implied a pejorative connotation,

Ferrer's use of the diminutive suffix '-*ita*', along with the plaintive question of the song's chorus, suggests some form of affection in the usage.

39. http://www.rockpaperscissors.biz/index.cfm/fuseaction/current.press_release/project_id/196.cfm

40. *Danzón* is a 'Cubanised' dance form, incorporating elements from European dances and Cuban forms such as the *Hanbanera*. *Danzón* was popular in Cuba from the mid 19th Century.

41. Sindo Garay was one of the luminaries of the original *trova* (Cuban folk song) movement in Cuba. Many of his songs have entered into Cuban heritage (the most famous perhaps '*Perla Marina*'), and Garay is called one of the 'four greats of *trova*'.

42. Ñico Saquito is another *trova* composer, famed for his wit and humour. Jose Martí is a national hero in Cuba, canonised by the revolution. He was a writer, political thinker and fought in the war of independence against Spain.

43. '*filín*' – a Cubanised pronunciation of the English word 'feeling' – is a musical genre from 1940s Cuba. Often defined as an intermediary between '*trova*' of the late 19th Century (the music of Sindo Garay etc) and '*nueva trova*' of the 1960s (the music of Silvio Rodriguez etc).

44. '*Coro de clave*' was an urban music popular in Matanzas and Havana at the end of the 19th Century.

45. Yaguajay – Ferrer's birthplace - is a town in central Cuba.

Bibliography

Acosta, Leonardo (1990) 'The Problem of Music and its Dissemination in Cuba' In Manuel, Peter (ed.) Essays on Cuban Music. Lanham and London: University Press of Arizona

Águila, Gorki (2010) Interview with the author. Havana. May 20th

Agawu, Kofi (1995) 'The Invention of "African Rhythm"' Journal of the American Musicological Society Vol. 48, No. 3, pp. 380-395

Alexander, Jeffrey (2004) 'Towards a Theory of Cultural Trauma' in Alexander, Jeferey, Ron Eyerman, Bernhard Giesen, Neil J. Smelser and Piotr Sztompka (Eds.) (2004) 'Cultural Trauma and Collective Identity' Berkeley: University of California Press

Amaro, Nelson and Alejandro Portes (1972) 'Una Sociología del Exilio: Situación de los Grupos Cubanos en los Estados Unidos' Aportes 23 pp. 6-24

Attali, Jacques (2004) 'Noise and Politics' in Cox, Christopher and Daniel Warner (eds.) 'Audio Culture: Readings in Modern Music' New York: Continuum

Arango, Arturo (1997) 'To Write in Cuba, Today' South Atlantic Quarterly Duke University Press

Badiou, Alain (2001) 'An Essay on the Understanding of Evil' London and New York: Verso

Barker, Hugh and Yuval Taylor (2007) 'Faking it: The Quest for Authenticity in Popular Music' New York: W.W. Norton and co.

Berg, Mette Louise (2005) 'Localising Cubanness: Social Exclusion and Narratives of Belonging in Old Havana' in 'Caribbean Narratives' Fog Olwig, Karen and Besson, Jean (Eds.) London: Macmillan

Bhabha, Homi (1990) 'The Third Space' in 'Identity: Community, Culture, Difference' Rutherford, Jonathan (Ed.) London: Lawrence and Wishart

Bhabha, Homi (1994) 'The Location of Culture' London and New

York: Roudledge

Biddle, Ian (2009) 'Visitors, or the Political Ontology of Noise' Radical Musicology 4

Borges, Jorge Luis (2004) 'The Aleph' in 'The Aleph and Other Stories' London: Penguin

Buckwater-Arias, James (2005) 'Reinscribing the Aesthetic: Cuban Narratives and Post-Soviet Cultural Politics' in PLMA Vol. 120, No. 2 (Mar. 2005) pp. 362-374

Bruner, Edward (1986) 'Ethnography as Narrative' in 'The Anthropology of Experience' Turner, V.W. and E.M. Bruner (Eds.), pp. 139-55 Urbana: University of Illinois Press

Castro, Fidel (1961) 'Words to the Intellectuals' Havana: National Cultural Council (translation: http://lanic.utexas.edu/project/castro/db/1961/19610630.html: Accessed 25/11/11)

Chacón Núñez, Lourdes (2009) 'Internalised Racism' in 'Islas' Vol.4 #11 (Jan. 2009) Florida

Edensor, Tim (2002) 'National Identity, Popular Culture and Everyday Life' Oxford and New York: Berg

Escondida Press Release (2002), 'Pedro Luis Ferrer Reinvents Cuban Music: Revolutionary Songs On His Own Terms' http://www.rockpaperscissors.biz/index.cfm/fuseaction/current.press_release/project_id/196.cfm (Accessed 12/02/10)

Fernandez, Raúl A (1994) 'The Course of U.S. Cuban Music: Margin and Mainstream' in 'Cuban Studies 24' Santí, Enrico Mario (Ed.) Pittsburgh: Pittsburgh University Press

Ferrer, Pedro Luis (2010) Interview with the author. Havana. May 22nd

Feracho, Lesley (2000) 'Arrivals and Farewells: The Dynamics of Cuban Home space through African Mythology in Two Eleggua Poems by Nancy Morejón' in 'Hispania', Vol. 83, No.1 (March 2003) pp.51-58 New York: American Association of Teachers of Spanish and Portuguese

Fernandes, Sujatha (2003) 'Fear of a Black Nation: Local Rappers,

Transnational Crossings and State Power in Contemporary Cuba' in 'Anthropology Quarterly', Vol. 76, No. 4 (Autumn 2003) pp. 575 – 608 Washington DC: George Washington University Press

Fernandes, Sujatha (2006) *'Cuba Represent! Cuban Arts, State Power, and the Making of New Revolutionary Cultures'* Durham: Duke University Press

de la Fuente, Alejandro (2001) *'A Nation For All: Race, Inequality and Politics in Twentieth- Century Cuba'* Chapel Hill: The University of North Carolina Press

García Freyre, Laura (2008) *'Porno Para Ricardo: Rock, "Analchy" and Transition'* in Changing Cuba/Changing World March 13-15, 2008 New York: City University of New York

Garcia, Maria Cristina (1996) *'Havana USA: Cuban Exiles and Cuban Americans in South Florida, 1959-1994'* Berkeley: University of California Press

Gellner, Ernest (1988) *'Nations and nationalism'* (4th edition) Oxford: Blackwell

Gott, Richard (2004) *'Cuba: A New History'* New Haven and London: Yale University Press

Hansing, Katrin (2007) *'Rasta, Race and Revolution: The Emergence and Development of the Rastafari Movement in Socialist Cuba'* Münster: Lit Verlag

Hernández, Rafael and Haroldo Dilla (1992) *'Political Culture and Popular Participation'* in 'The Cuban Revolution into the 1990s edited by the Centro de Estudios Sobre América' Boulder: Westview Press (translated by Jennifer Dugan Abbassi and Jean Días)

Huxley, Aldous (1944) *'The Perennial Philosophy'* New York: Harper and Brothers

Kapcia, Antoni (2000) *'Cuba: Island of Dreams'* Oxford and New York: Berg

Kapcia, Antoni (2005) *'Havana: The Making of Cuban Culture'* Oxford and New York: Berg

Lefebvre, Henri (1991) 'The Production of Space' Oxford: Blackwell

Lefebvre, Henri (2004) 'Rhythmanalysis: Space, Time and Everyday Life' London and New York: Continuum (translated by Stuart Elden and Gerald Moore)

Malinowski, Bronislaw (1939) 'Introduction' in Fernando Ortiz 'Cuban Counterpoint: Tobacco and Sugar' pp. lvii - lxv Durham: Duke University Press (translated by Harriet de Onís)

Massey, Doreen (1995) 'The Conceptualisation of Place' in D. Massey and P. Jess (eds.) 'A Place in the World? Places, Cultures and Globalisation' Oxford: Oxford University Press

Massey, Doreen (1998) 'The Spatial Construction of Youth Cultures' in Tracey Skelton and Gill Valentine (eds.) 'Cool Places: Geographies of Youth Cultures' London: Routledge

Masvidal, Mario (2007) Interview with Freemuse (Jan. 2007): www.freemuse.org/sw16482.asp (Accessed 05/10/09)

Maza, Eric (2010) 'Cuban Punk Rockers Gorki and Gill Used Music to Take on Castro' Miami New Times, 24/06/10. http://www. miaminewtimes.com/2010-06-24/music/cuban-punk-rockers-gorki-and-gil-used-music-to-take-on-castro/ (accessed 03/03/11)

Moles, Abraham (1968) 'Information Theory and Esthetic Perception' Urbana: University of Illinois Press (translated by Joel E Cohen)

Moore, Robin (2003) 'Transformations in Cuban Nueva Trova 1965-95' Ethnomusicology 47 (1) (Winter 2003) 1-41

Moore, Robin (1997) 'Nationalising Blackness: Afrocubanismo and Artistic Revolution in Havana 1920 - 1940' Pittsburgh; University of Pittsburgh Press

Moses, Catherine (2000) 'Real Life in Castro's Cuba' Wilmington: Scholarly Resources Inc.

Movimiento Libertario Cubano (MLC) (2008) 'Cuba: interview with Porno Para Ricardo' (June 18th 2008) http:// www.indymedia.org.uk/en/2008/06/401490.html (Accessed 18/11/09)

Navarro, Lygia (2005) *'Underground Man: An Interview With Pedro Luis Ferrer'* http://motherjones.com/media/2005/06/underground-man-interview-pedro-luis-ferrer (Accessed 12/06/09)

Pacini Hernandez, Deborah (1998) *'Dancing with the Enemy: Cuban Popular Music, Race, Authenticity and the World Music Landscape'* in 'Latin American Perspectives' Issue 100, Vol. 25 No.3 May 1998 pp. 110- 125 London: Sage

Pacini Hernandez, Deborah and Reebee Garofalo (1999) *'Hip hop in Havana: Rap, Race and National Identity in Contemporary Cuba'* in 'Journal of Popular Music Studies' 11/12 (1999/2000) pp. 18 -47 Oxford: Blackwell Publishing

Pacini Hernandez and Reebee Garofalo (2004) *'Between Rock and a Hard Place: Negotiating Rock in Revolutionary Cuba 1960 - 1980'* in 'Rockin' Las Américas: The Global Politics of Rock in Latin/o America ' Deborah Pacini Hernandez, Hector Fernández L'Hoeste and Eric Zolov (eds.) Pittsburg: University of Pittsburg Press

O'Reilly Herrera, Andrea (ed.) (2001) *'Remembering Cuba: Legacy of a Diaspora'* Austin: University of Texas Press

Pedraza-Bailey, Silvia (1985) *'Cuba's Exiles: Portrait of a Refugee Migration'* International Migration Review, Vol. 19, No. 1 (Spring 1985) pp.4-34

Pérez, Lisandro (2008) *'Reflections on the Future of Cuba'* in Louis Perez (ed.) 'Cuban Studies 39' pp.85-91

Perez, Louis A (1999) *'On Becoming Cuban: Identity, Nationality and Culture'* California: University of California Press

Perez, Louis A. (2003) *'Cuba and the United States: Ties of Singular Intimacy'* (Third Edition) Athens and London: University of Georgia Press

Perez, Louis A (2006) *'Cuba: Between Reform and Revolution'* Oxford: Oxford University Press

Perna, Vincenzo (2005) *'Timba: The Sound of the Cuban Crisis'* Aldershot: Ashgate

Placák, Petr (2006) *'Llegó la Hora de Llamar las Cosas por su Nombre'*

(*It's Time to Call Things by Their Name'*) http://www.cubaen-cuentro.com/entrevistas/articulos/llego-la-hora-de-llamar-las-cosas-por-su-nombre-23885 (Accessed 12/03/11)

Rodríguez, Yusimí (2011) 'To Express My Ideas and Have Them Heard: Interview With Raudel Collazo Pedroso' Havana Times: http://www.havanatimes.org/?p=37846 (accessed 28/11/11

Silva Brenneman, Eric (2004) *'Havana and Miami: A Music Censorship Sandwich'* in 'Shoot the Singer: Music Censorship Today' Marie Korpe (ed.) London, New York: Zed Books

Soja, Edward W. (1996) *'Thirdspace: Journeys to Los Angeles and Other Real-and-Imagined Places'* Cambridge, Mass.: Blackwell

Suárez, Michel (2003) *'Prohibido Escuchar'* in 'Cuba Encuentro', 23rd Jan, 2003 (translated by Mariley Reinoso Olivera)

Suchlichi, Jamie (2000) *'Castro's Cuba: Continuity Instead of Change'* in Susan Kaufman Purcell and David J. Rothkopf (eds.) 'Cuba: The Contours of Change' London and Boulder: Lynne Reinner Publishers

Sztompka, Piotr (2004) *'The Trauma of Social Change'* in Alexander, Jeferey, Ron Eyerman, Bernhard Giesen, Neil J. Smelser and Piotr Sztompka (Eds.) (2004) *'Cultural Trauma and Collective Identity'* Berkeley: University of California Press

Tacchi, Jo (1998) *'Radio Texture: Between Self and Other'* in D. Miller (ed.) *'material Cultures: Why Some Things Matter'* London: UCL Press

Discography/Filmography

Bosch, Carles and Josep Maria Domènech (2002) *'Balseros'* Bausan Films

Cuoma, Alessio and de Nooij, Sander (2008) *'¡Cuba Rebelión!'* Column Films

Escuadrón Patriota (2010) *'El Legado'* Champions Records

Ferrer, Pedro Luis (1999) *'Pedro Luis Ferrer'* Atlantic/WEA

Ferrer, Pedro Luis (2005) *'Rustico'* La Escondida

Ferrer, Pedro Luis Ferrer (2006) *'Natural'* La Escondida

Ferrer, Padro Luis (2010) *'Tangible'* Ultra Records

Porno Para Ricardo (2002) *'Rock Para Las Masas (Cárnicas)'* Havana, Cuba: La Paja Records

Porno Para Ricardo (2006a) *'A Mi No Me Gusta La Política, Pero Yo Le Gusta A Ella Compañero'* Havana, Cuba: La Paja Records

Porno Para Ricardo (2006b) *'Soy Porno, Soy Popular'* Havana, Cuba: La Paja Records

Porno Para Ricardo (2009) *'El Disco Rojo Desteñido'* La Paja Records

Puebla, Carlos (2004) *'Cuba Si, Yankees No'* Gran Via-U

Trueba, Fernando, Tono Errando and Javier Mariscal, (2010) *'Chico & Rita'* CinemaNX

Varela, Carlos (1989) *'Jalisco Park'* Eligeme

Varela, Carlos (2005) *'Los Hijos de Guillermo Tell Vol. 1'* Unicornio

Various (1992) *'Cuban Classics 3: Diablo al Infierno!'* Luaka Bop

Acknowledgements

Pedro Luis Ferrer, Gorki Águila, Ciro Díaz, and Raudel Collazo; impassioned music that has become such an integral part of my own identity.

Mum, Dad, Charlotte and Will; consistent encouragement and necessary mickey-taking.

The Astleys, The Macdonalds, The Yules; a lifetime of family parties, in-jokes and laughter.

My Cuban family; accepting me into a loving and immensely talented family, despite the barriers of language and culture.

Nanette de Jong; tireless support, encouragement and infectious enthusiasm.

Ian Biddle and Richard Elliott; a radical and challenging academic environment.

E.A.R.; solidarity, the North-East Passage, and cups of tea.

Paco and Arancha; wonderful nights of great food, conversation and music.

Alex Niven; a true friend.

Mariley Reinoso Olivera - my wife - without whom this work would not exist, and my life would be immeasurably poorer.

Contemporary culture has eliminated both the concept of the public and the figure of the intellectual. Former public spaces – both physical and cultural – are now either derelict or colonized by advertising. A cretinous anti-intellectualism presides, cheerled by expensively educated hacks in the pay of multinational corporations who reassure their bored readers that there is no need to rouse themselves from their interpassive stupor. The informal censorship internalized and propagated by the cultural workers of late capitalism generates a banal conformity that the propaganda chiefs of Stalinism could only ever have dreamt of imposing. Zer0 Books knows that another kind of discourse – intellectual without being academic, popular without being populist – is not only possible: it is already flourishing, in the regions beyond the striplit malls of so called mass media and the neurotically bureaucratic halls of the academy. Zer0 is committed to the idea of publishing as a making public of the intellectual. It is convinced that in the unthinking, blandly consensual culture in which we live, critical and engaged theoretical reflection is more important than ever before.